A-level Study Guide

Physical Education and Sport

Revised and updated for 2008 by

Michael Hill

...ision Express

Series Consultants: Geoff Black and Stuart Wall

Project Manager: Hywel Evans

Pearson Education Limited

Edinburgh Gate, Harlow

Essex CM20 2JE, England

www.pearsoned.co.uk

and Associated Companies throughout the world

British Library Cataloguing-in-Publication Data

A catalogue entry for this title is available from the British Library.

ISBN 978-1-4082-0663-8

First published 2006

New edition 2008

Reprinted 2008

Set by Juice Creative Ltd

Printed and bound by Ashford Colour Press Ltd, Gosport, Hampshire

Contents

How to use this book

Specification map
Provides a quick and easy overview of the topics that you need to cover for the specification you are studying (see pages 6–7)

Exam themes
At the beginning of each chapter, these give a quick overview of the key themes that will be covered in the exam

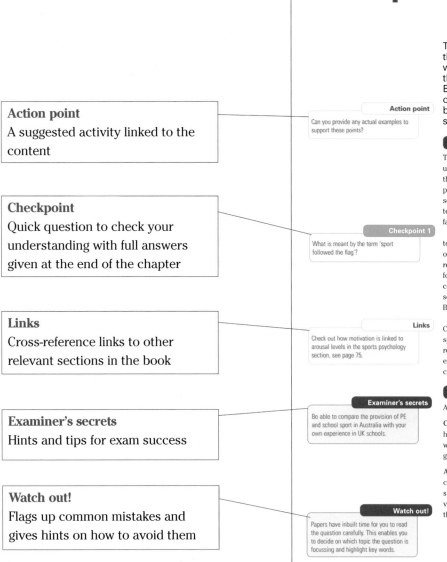

Exam themes

- The structure and function of the skeletal system

- The structure of muscles and their role in creating movement

The impact of athleticism on society

The emergence of a modern form of sport through the public school system of the nineteenth century was to have a profound effect on the spread of sport throughout society, both in Britain and throughout the British Empire. It sowed the seeds of the rationalisation of sport, in which sports were codified and regulated by governing bodies, and the boys who left the school spread the cult of manly games across the world.

Exploring the games ethic

The missionaries, ambassadors, generals and businessmen initially used games for their own recreation but then began to pass them onto the indigenous peoples of the colonies and other trading nations. The philosophy was to develop some of the moral characteristics that were so important to the English gentleman. Central to this philosophy were team games, as these proved to be the perfect medium for transferring favourable virtues that made up the games cult.

Through these sports, the indigenous people could learn the basic tools of imperial command: courage, endurance, discipline, loyalty and obedience. Cricket supplied a new conception of chivalry that seemed reflect exactly the national characteristics of Victorian England. Rugby football promoted values more suited to imperialism: fearlessness and control. In summary, the games developed and promoted by the public schools could produce both the confidence to lead among the ex-pat British and the compulsion to follow among the indigenous people.

Imperialism was felt by most people in Britain to be a very worthwhile Christian activity. They were moralising and civilising the world – with sport an essential element of this. There were also more sound political reasons for the creation and maintenance of the Empire: trade, security, emigration, prestige and, in the case of Australia, somewhere to dump criminals or social misfits.

Public school sport travels the world

An effective way of summarising this impact is CAT PUICCA.

C – colonial Many public-school boys took up posts in the colonial service helping to administer and govern the Empire's many colonies. They took with them their sporting kit. Initially, they played among themselves but gradually introduced the sports and games to the indigenous population.

A – army Another career for many public-school boys was as commissioned officers in the armed forces. Initially, the officers would sports as a recreation to fill in long hours, but the social control and value of keeping the working-class soldiers occupied were not lost on them. This played an important part in spreading the cult still further.

Action point
A suggested activity linked to the content

Action point
Can you provide any actual examples to support these points?

Checkpoint
Quick question to check your understanding with full answers given at the end of the chapter

Checkpoint 1
What is meant by the term 'sport followed the flag'?

Links
Cross-reference links to other relevant sections in the book

Links
Check out how motivation is linked to arousal levels in the sports psychology section, see page 75.

Examiner's secrets
Hints and tips for exam success

Examiner's secrets
Be able to compare the provision of PE and school sport in Australia with your own experience in UK schools.

Watch out!
Flags up common mistakes and gives hints on how to avoid them

Watch out!
Papers have inbuilt time for you to read the question carefully. This enables you to decide on which topic the question is focussing and highlight key words.

Topic checklist

A topic overview of the content covered and how it matches to the specification you are studying

Revision checklist

Allows you to monitor your progress and revise the areas where you are not confident

Topic checklist

	Edexcel		AQA		OCR		WJEC	
	AS	A2	AS	A2	AS	A2	AS	A2
The skeletal and muscular system	O		O		O		O	
Motion and movement	O		O		O		O	

By the end of this chapter you should be able to:

1	Describe the structure and function of the skeletal system.	Confident	Not confident **Revise** page 4
2	Discuss the definitions and laws of motion.	Confident	Not confident **Revise** page 5

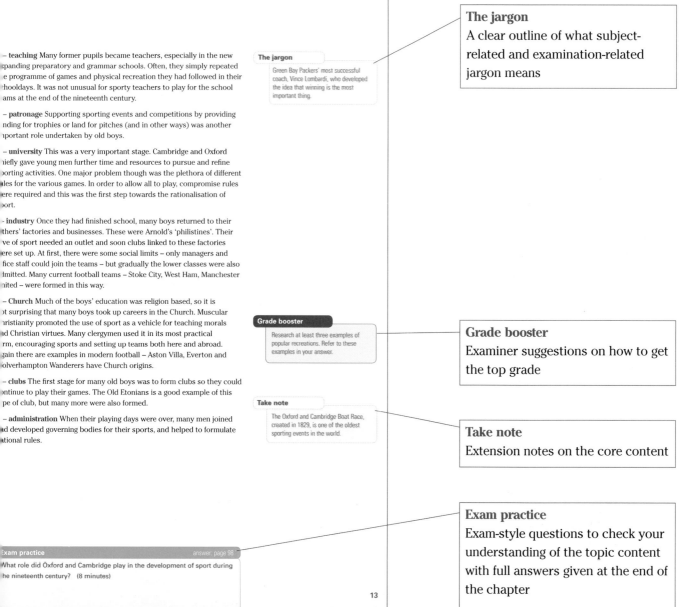

The jargon
A clear outline of what subject-related and examination-related jargon means

– teaching Many former pupils became teachers, especially in the new expanding preparatory and grammar schools. Often, they simply repeated the programme of games and physical recreation they had followed in their schooldays. It was not unusual for sporty teachers to play for the school teams at the end of the nineteenth century.

– patronage Supporting sporting events and competitions by providing funding for trophies or land for pitches (and in other ways) was another important role undertaken by old boys.

– university This was a very important stage. Cambridge and Oxford chiefly gave young men further time and resources to pursue and refine sporting activities. One major problem though was the plethora of different rules for the various games. In order to allow all to play, compromise rules were required and this was the first step towards the rationalisation of sport.

– industry Once they had finished school, many boys returned to their fathers' factories and businesses. These were Arnold's 'philistines'. Their love of sport needed an outlet and soon clubs linked to these factories were set up. At first, there were some social limits – only managers and office staff could join the teams – but gradually the lower classes were also admitted. Many current football teams – Stoke City, West Ham, Manchester United – were formed in this way.

– Church Much of the boys' education was religion based, so it is not surprising that many boys took up careers in the Church. Muscular Christianity promoted the use of sport as a vehicle for teaching morals and Christian virtues. Many clergymen used it in its most practical form, encouraging sports and setting up teams both here and abroad. Again there are examples in modern football – Aston Villa, Everton and Wolverhampton Wanderers have Church origins.

– clubs The first stage for many old boys was to form clubs so they could continue to play their games. The Old Etonians is a good example of this type of club, but many more were also formed.

– administration When their playing days were over, many men joined and developed governing bodies for their sports, and helped to formulate national rules.

The jargon

Green Bay Packers' most successful coach, Vince Lombardi, who developed the idea that winning is the most important thing.

Grade booster

Research at least three examples of popular recreations. Refer to these examples in your answer.

Take note

The Oxford and Cambridge Boat Race, created in 1829, is one of the oldest sporting events in the world.

Grade booster
Examiner suggestions on how to get the top grade

Take note
Extension notes on the core content

Exam practice
Exam-style questions to check your understanding of the topic content with full answers given at the end of the chapter

Exam practice   answer: page 98

What role did Oxford and Cambridge play in the development of sport during the nineteenth century? (8 minutes)

13

Specification map

Anatomy and physiology	The skeletal and muscular system
	Motion and movement
	Laws of motion
	The cardiovascular system
	The role of blood in transporting oxygen and carbon dioxide
	The respiratory system
	Nutrition and sport
	Fitness training and testing
Skill acquisition	Characteristics and types of skills
	Memory
	Motivation
	Feedback
The social contemporary study of sport	Sport, leisure and recreation: key concepts
	Sport and culture
	Sport in advanced societies
	Élite sport
	Ethics and values in high-level sport
	Sport and mass participation
	Factors affecting participation
	The Olympic Games
	Issues at the Olympics
	Sport, sponsorship and the media
Exercise physiology	Energy concepts
	Fatigue, recovery and training
	Aerobic capacity and strength training
	Flexibility
Sports psychology	Sports psychology and its effects on the individual performer
	Sports psychology and its effects on group performance
	Mental preparation for sport
	Effects and consequences of competition
Historical study of physical education and sport	Sport before 1800
	Sport in the English public schools
	The impact of athleticism on society
	Sport after 1800 – the rational phase
	The development of PE in British state schools 1870–1944
The comparative study of global sporting systems	Sport in North American cultures
	Administration of sport in North American cultures
	Mass participation and élite sport in the USA
	Sport in New World culture – Australia
	Administration of sport in Australia
	Mass participation and élite sport in Australia

	Edexcel		AQA		OCR		WJEC	
	AS	A2	AS	A2	AS	A2	AS	A2
	○		○		○		○	
	○		○		○		○	
	○		○		○		○	
	○		○		○		○	
	○		○		○		○	
	○		○		○		○	
	○		○		○		○	
	○		○		○		○	
	Not examined		○		○		○	
			○		○		○	
		Not examined		●	○			●
			○		○		○	
	○		○		○		○	
					○			
		●			○			●
	○			●	○		○	
	○	●		●	○	●	○	
	○	●	○		○		○	●
	○		○		○		○	●
	○		○		○		○	●
	○		○		○			●
	○		○		○			
		●		●		●	○	
		●		●		●	○	
	○	●	○	●		●	○	
	○		○	●				●
		●		●		●		●
		●		●		●		●
		●		●		●		●
		●		●		●		●
	○					●		
	○		○			●	○	
	○		○			●	○	
	○		○			●	○	
	○		○			●	○	
		●		●		●		●
		●		●		●		●
		●		●		●		●
		●				●		
		●				●		●
		●				●		●

Anatomy and physiology

In this chapter we revise the anatomy and physiology of the human body with reference to exercise and movement. Traditionally this is one of the most difficult areas of the exam and needs thorough revision. The main focus should be on the systems that play a significant role in producing movement on the body – the skeletal, muscular, cardiovascular and respiratory systems. Some of the A-level specifications also require candidates to study nutrition in sport as well as fitness testing and training.

The key to exam success in this section is having a thorough understanding of the structure and function of the key body parts and systems, and then applying your points to sporting examples.

Exam themes

- The structure and function of the skeletal system
- The structure of muscles and their role in creating movement
- Movement production and control
- The laws of motion
- The structure and function of the cardiovascular system
- The role of blood in transporting oxygen and carbon dioxide
- The structure and role of the respiratory system
- Nutrition and sport
- Fitness training and testing

Topic checklist

	Edexcel		AQA		OCR		WJEC	
	AS	A2	AS	A2	AS	A2	AS	A2
The skeletal and muscular system	O		O		O		O	
Motion and movement	O		O		O		O	
Laws of motion	O		O		O		O	
The cardiovascular system	O		O		O		O	
The role of blood in transporting oxygen and carbon dioxide	O		O		O		O	
The respiratory system	O		O		O		O	
Nutrition and sport	O		O		O		O	
Fitness training and testing	O		O		O		O	

The skeletal and muscular system

The human skeleton is made up of a combination of bones, joints and cartilage. It has two parts, an **axial** or central part and an **appendicular** part which is attached to the central axial skeleton.

The skeleton has a nummber of functions, it:

→ provides **shape**; supports the body in the correct **posture**; **supports** the internal organs; **protects** the body.

→ provides sites of **muscle attachment**; creates **levers**; enables us to make **movements**; **produces** blood cells.

Joints

The reasons we are able to move when we play sport is because of our joints, specifically in sport the movable synovial joints. You need to be able to describe and discuss the types of movement that can occur at the following joints.

→ Wrist   Radio-ulnar   Elbow   Shoulder
→ Spine   Hip   Knee   Ankle

Synovial joints allow a great range of movement, formed where a fluid-filled cavity surrounds the meeting of two bones, the ends of which are coated with articular cartilage which acts as a shock absorber.

Ligaments of tough, inelastic connective tissue hold the bones together. They act to prevent any unwanted movement. Tendons, made of fibrous connective tissue, attach the muscles to the bones.

Joints can undergo a number of different movements – you will need to understand the meaning of each movement type, be able to apply these to a range of sporting activities and be able to identify the range of movements possible at each joint.

Movement term	Description
Flexion	Decrease in angle between the two bones
Extention	Increase in the angle between two bones
Abduction	Movement of a limb away from an imaginary vertical line down the middle of the body
Adduction	Movement of a limb towards the imaginary mid-line of the body
Rotation	Circular movement
Circumduction	A combination of flexion, extention, abduction, adduction and rotation

Checkpoint 1

Describe four functions of the human skeleton.

Checkpoint 2

What characteristics of synovial joints allow a great range of movement?

Checkpoint 3

Explain the differing roles of ligaments and tendons.

Action point

See if you can give a sporting example for each of the movement types identified.

Muscles and movement

Muscle tissue has four main characteristics:

→ excitability
→ contractility
→ extensibility
→ elasticity.

This means that muscles:

→ react to a stimulus
→ contract and apply force
→ stretch and return to their original length
→ have involuntary control.

Grade booster

Be able to explain how the structure and function of the skeletal muscle system aid movement in sport.

Triceps
Agonist

Biceps
Antagonist

Muscles can be classified according to the fibre arrangement around the tendon as follows:

→ **Fusiform** – where the fibres run the length of the muscle, a type of muscle designed for mobility.
→ **Pennate** – where the fibres are structured in a fan shape, a type of muscle designed for strength.

Each actual muscle consists of a bundle of fibres contained by a layer of connective tissue known as the **epimysium**. Its role is to protect the muscle and help it slide smoothly past nearby muscles, bones and other organs as it changes in length.

Inside the epimysium, the muscle is further grouped into bundles. Each of these is divided by thinner layers of connective tissue containing blood vessels and nerve fibres.

Skeletal muscle has a striped appearance due to the microscopic fibres called **myofibrils** which they contain. These myofibrils are made up of alternating rows of two basic protein filaments called **actin** and **myosin**, which resemble the teeth of interlocking combs. According to the sliding filament theory, small projections on the myosin filaments allow the protein filaments to slide past each other as the muscle changes in length.

Checkpoint 4

What is the role of the epimysium surrounding the muscle fibres?

Exam practice answers: page 28

Explain how the functions of the skeleton facilitate physical activity.

(8 minutes)

Motion and movement

If the skeletal system creates a framework for the body, it is the muscles that maintain our body shape and enable us to move our body parts. They are therefore extremely important when we play sport.

The structure of skeletal muscle

Muscles are usually attached to two or more different bones so that when they contract, movement occurs. Fibrous connective tissues called tendons attach muscles to bones at sites called the point of **origin** and the point of **insertion**. Where a muscle is attached to a bone, a lever system is formed.

A feature of muscle fibres is that they can contract, or pull, against the skeleton. Most muscles are long and thin, but when they contract they get **shorter** and **thicker** – this is called concentric contraction. What muscles cannot do is push, because muscles cannot push. To make joints work, the muscles are arranged in pairs called **antagonistic pairs**. The best example of antagonistic pairs of muscles are the biceps and triceps. At the elbow, in order to bend the arm, the **biceps** contract (shorten) while the **triceps** relax (lengthen).

There are two other connected terms which you should know:

1 Fixators are any other muscles situated near the point of origin of the prime mover, which act to stabilise the body part, so that only the end at the point of insertion will move.
2 Synergists are another muscle actively working to help the prime mover to cause a movement.

The study of muscles in sport is mainly focussed on when they are in a state of contraction. This can happen in a number of different ways. **Concentric** contraction can occur when a muscle shortens in length and develops tension. **Eccentric** contraction involves the development of tension while the muscle is being lengthened. **Isometric** contraction occurs when the muscle develops tension but does not change in length. Finally isokinetic contraction is a special situation in which the muscle is changing in length but at a constant rate.

Skeletal muscle is further divided into three main fibre types:

Type	Description
Type I (slow oxidative)	A type of muscle fibre characterised by a relatively slow contraction, making it suitable for low-power and long-duration activities usually referred to as aerobic.
Type IIa (fast oxidative glycolytic or FOG)	Have a higher oxidative capacity than type IIb and are often associated with short high-intensity endurance events such as the 400m in athletics.
Type IIb (fast glycolytic or FG)	Have the highest level of phosphocreatine and special enzymes, giving the highest glycolytic capacity and are associated with explosive events such as the start of the 100m sprint start.

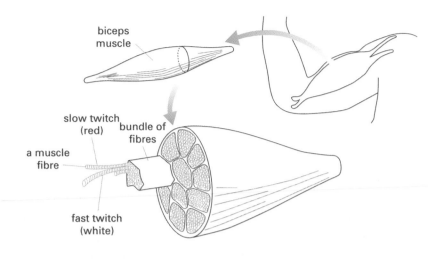

biceps muscle

slow twitch (red)

bundle of fibres

a muscle fibre

fast twitch (white)

Movement production and control

The muscular system allows us to maintain our body position and move body parts. The body's nervous system enables us to coordinate and control our movements. The nervous system consists of the brain, spinal cord, nerve fibre and effector and receptor organs. Nerve cells or neurones carry the information to and from the spinal cord and brain; sensory neurones receive information from the receptor organs and transmit impulses to the brain, where the information is processed, then motor neurones transmit impulses from the brain to the effector organs such as the muscles.

Neurones have two main sections. Dentrites receive impulses from other nerve cells. These impulses are then transmitted along the axon. At the end of the axon the impulses divide into branches which form synapses with other neurones. Neurones are not actually connected to each other but are separated by tiny gaps known as synapses.

Impulses are able to cross this gap via the release of a chemical substance called acetylcholine, which allows an impulse to travel through the nervous system at great speed.

Within a muscle, one motor neurone will stimulate a number of muscle fibres (up to 2000 fibres). Generally, small muscles capable of precise movements are composed of motor units with few muscle fibres, whereas muscles that create large or gross movements contain motor units with a large number of muscle fibres. Each motor unit obeys the all-or-none law: all the fibres in a single motor unit receive the same neural stimulation, so they all act maximally when the threshold of stimulation is met.

The force exerted by a muscle is dependent on the number of motor units recruited and the frequency of the stimulation. Together, this is referred to as the gradation of contraction. Generally, the more units recruited and/or the greater the frequency of stimulation, the greater the tension developed by the muscle and the greater the force the muscle can apply.

Checkpoint 1

List the structures that make up the body's nervous system.

The jargon

Synapse – the main role of the synapse is to convey action potential between neurones.

Checkpoint 2

Explain what is meant by the all-or-none law.

The jargon

Together the *neurone* and the *fibres* it stimulates make up what is called the *motor unit*.

The jargon

All-or-none law: a neurone or muscle fibre either responds completely or not at all to a stimulus.

Checkpoint 3

What structures make up a motor unit?

Checkpoint 4

Explain the difference in function between effector organs and receptor organs.

Exam practice   answers: page 28

Explain what is meant by the terms Type I, Type IIa and Type IIb muscle fibres and comment on their relevance to particular types of sporting activity.

(10 minutes)

Laws of motion

*Every body continues
in its state of rest, or
of uniform motion in
a straight line, except
in so far as it may be
compelled by impressed
forces to change that
state.*

Newton's first law of motion

Take note

Pure linear motion is rarely seen in most sports events but it can often be apparent in sporting actions such as sprinting.

Example

The most common sporting example of Newton's third law is a sprinter's start blocks. When the sprinter pushes out of the blocks there is a resultant opposite and equal force pushing the sprinter forward off the blocks.

In sport, motion is produced only when force is applied. The main sources of this force are:

→ internal – the muscular system of the athlete contracting to produce force
→ external – this could include gravity, friction of fluid or surface or resistance of the air.

Types of motion in sport

Motion is of two kinds:

→ **Linear motion** is the progression of a body in a straight line with all its parts moving the same distance, in the same direction and at the same speed.
→ **Angular motion** is the more common type, where a body rotates about a fixed point.

Often, in sport the most efficient movement requires a combination of linear and angular motion.

Newton's laws of motion are fundamental to an understanding of how these elements combine to effect sporting performance.

Newton's first law of motion, the law of inertia, states that an object will remain at rest unless acted on by an external source. Also, if the object is moving, then it will do so in the same direction and at the same velocity unless acted upon by an external force.

Newton's second law of motion, the law of acceleration, states that when a body is acted on by a force, its resulting change in momentum takes place in the direction in which the force is applied and is in proportion to the force causing it and inversely proportional to its mass. This is often expressed by the formulae $a = f/m$.

Newton's third law of motion, the law of reaction, states that for every action there is an equal and opposite reaction. Therefore, when one object exerts a force on another, there will be an equal force exerted in the opposite direction by the second object on the first.

Measuring and presenting linear motion

The three main components linked to linear motion are:

→ **Speed** is distance travelled per unit time measured in ms⁻¹. Speed is a scalar quantity and is calculated thus: speed = distance/time

→ **Velocity** is the rate at which a body moves. It is a vector quantity in that it possesses both magnitude and direction. It is measured in ms⁻¹ and is calculated thus: velocity = displacement/time

→ **Acceleration** is the rate of change in velocity and is therefore a vector quantity. It is measured in ms⁻¹ and is calculated thus: acceleration = change in velocity/time taken to change.

Often, linear motion qualities in sport are presented as graphic descriptions:

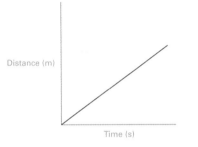

This graph represents steady speed

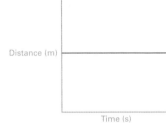

This graph with a horizontal line represents stationary

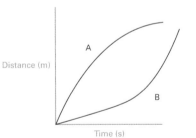

On this graph, line A represents deceleration and line B represents acceleration

The jargon

Scalar quantity is a physical quantity that is described completely in terms of its magnitude.

Checkpoint 1

Explain the difference between scalar and vector qualities.

The jargon

Velocity is the rate at which a body moves. It is a vector quantity in that it possesses both magnitude and direction.

The jargon

Displacement is the distance an object has moved in a given direction.

Checkpoint 2

How do we calculate acceleration?

Checkpoint 3

What are the correct units of measurement for speed, velocity and acceleration?

Action point

Make sure you know the correct units for speed, velocity and acceleration.

Checkpoint 4

What does a horizontal line on a distance *v* time graph represent?

Exam practice   answers: page 28

1   In sport, people and objects rarely travel at constant speed. Sketch and label four separate distance *v* time graphs showing the following:
   (i)   steady speed
   (ii) stationary
   (iii) acceleration
   (iv) deceleration. (10 minutes)

The cardiovascular system

The cardiovascular system is made up of the heart (cardio) and the circulatory network of the blood vessels (vascular). These two systems work together to ensure that the body receives a constant supply of blood. The heart is responsible for pumping blood around the body, to the lungs for oxygenation and to the rest of the body (tissues, organs and cells) for all bodily functions. This process includes sending oxygenated blood to the muscles for exercise. If we carry out a sustained programme of aerobic exercise, the cardiovascular system adapts and makes this transport of blood more efficient. This is a popular area for examination questions and it is well worth spending time making sure you understand all areas of this subject.

The heart

The heart is at the centre of the circulatory system, situated in the thorax between the lungs. It is a four-chambered pump as shown in the diagram below.

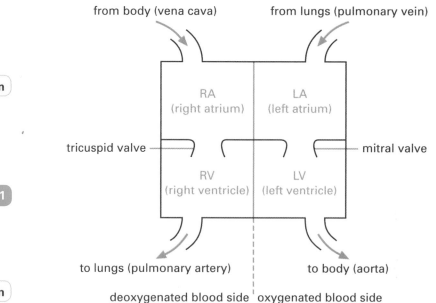

It consists largely of cardiac muscle, a specialised tissue that is capable of virtually unlimited rhythmical contraction and relaxation.

Blood flow

Deoxygenated blood enters the right side of the heart via the vena cava passing into the right atrium.

The right atrium contracts and forces the blood into the right ventricle through the tricuspid valves.

The ventricle then contracts; the same happens on the left-hand side since both sides of the heart contract simultaneously but the left ventricle wall is much thicker and greater force is generated when it

---

The jargon

The *tricuspid valve* has three flaps and prevents blood from flowing back into the right-hand side of the heart.

Checkpoint 1

Why is the left ventricle thicker walled than the right ventricle?

The jargon

Systole is a contraction phase of the cardiac cycle and *diastole* is the relaxation phase.

contracts, forcing blood initially into the aorta and then around the rest of the body.

The bicuspid valve prevents blood flowing back into the left-hand side of the heart.

Control of heart beat

The series of events that sees blood pass through the heart is referred to as the cardiac cycle.

The heart muscle is myogenic and does not need stimulation via the nervous system. The sinoatrial node (SAN) found in the right atrium acts as the heart's pacemaker. A wave of electrical stimulation arises from the SAN and then spreads over the two atria causing them to contract more or less at the same time. This stimulation reaches the atrioventricular node (AVN) found in the centre of the two atria and channels the impulse along the Purkinje tissue found in the walls of the ventricles. This stimulation is followed by the simultaneous contraction of the ventricles.

Heart rate (HR)

The rate at which the heart beats and the volume of blood pumped out at each beat can be varied.

Cardiac output (Q) = Heart rate (HR) × Stroke volume (SV)

The jargon

Stroke volume is the volume of blood ejected from the heart in one beat, measured in ml/beat.

Venous return

The heart can only pump as much blood as it receives. Any increase in cardiac output is dependent on the venous return increasing a similar amount of blood. During exercise, the effects of the 'muscle pump' means that there is an increase in the amount of blood returning to the heart. This causes the walls of the heart to stretch more than normal. This over-stretching stimulates the SA node to increase the heart rate and there is also an increase in the force of contraction. This effect is known as Starling's Law, and explains the relationship between an increase in stroke volume and an increase in venous return.

The jargon

Venous return is the volume of blood returning to the right atrium of the heart.

The jargon

The muscle pump is a term used to describe the increase in flow of blood back to the heart caused by the contracting of the skeletal muscles squeezing blood through the veins.

Control of blood supply

Changes to the cardiac output are effected through the autonomic nervous system:

→ Impulses from the **parasympathetic fibres** slow down the heart beat.
→ Impulses from the **sympathetic fibres** accelerate it.

The cardiac centre of the brain controls the parasympathetic and sympathetic impulses.

When we take part in physical activity, a number of changes occur in the cardiovascular system.

Checkpoint 2

What effect does stimulation of the parasympathetic system have on heart beat?

Checkpoint 3

What effect does stimulation of the sympathetic system have on heart beat?

Exam practice answers: page 28

Define venous return and explain how it is aided by exercise. (6 minutes)

The role of blood in transporting oxygen

Our muscles require energy in order to contract and enable us to produce physical movement. There are energy supplies within the working muscles but these are used up very quickly. Therefore we need a method of transporting oxygen into the muscles. About 8 per cent of our body weight is made up of blood – this important element is the substance in which various essential materials such as oxygen are transported around the body.

Transporting oxygen

When we exercise, the body needs to take in and transport more oxygen. In the capillaries around the alveoli, oxygen combines with haemoglobin and is transported as oxyhaemoglyobin to the tissues where the oxygen dissociates, due to the diffusion gradient. Within muscles, oxygen is transported by myoglobin to the mitochondria, where aerobic respiration takes place.

The effect of warming up and cooling down

A warm-up before strenuous physical activity has a direct effect on the cardiovascular system.

Vasodilation leads to:

→ increase in oxygen flow to the muscles
→ increase in temperature
→ increase in enzyme activity
→ decrease in blood viscosity
→ oxygen dissociates from haemoglobin ore readily.

The purpose of a cool-down is to help the body return to its normal state as soon as possible. A thorough cool-down routine will help keep the blood flow high, washing out all the waste products the muscles have produced, preventing blood pooling and helping to replenish the fuel stores.

Blood pressure

Blood pressure is the pressure needed to pump blood around the body. The average BP reading for an adult (measured using a sphygmomanometer) is 120/80mmHg. The first number represents systolic pressure when the heart forcefully ejects blood. The second figure represents diastolic pressure when the heart relaxes. If a person's blood pressure is consistently above 140/90mmHg, they are said to be suffering from hypertension and this can become a problem if left untreated. The heart has to work too hard and becomes inefficient, and this can commonly lead to a number of cardiovascular diseases including strokes and heart attacks. BP values can be affected by a number of factors such as age (arteries in older people are less elastic), stress and tension, diet and exercise.

and carbon dioxide

The effects of exercise on blood

A sustained programme of continuous or aerobic training can result in an increase of up to 8 per cent in blood volume. The corresponding increase in red blood cells means that more oxygen can be transported around the body to the muscles. Another method of increasing the number of red blood cells in the body is to train at altitude. At high altitude, the blood oxygen levels decrease, stimulating the body to produce more red blood cells.

The increased demand for oxygen in the working muscles causes an increase in heart rate. This is also helped by the release of the hormone adrenaline.

This increase in heart rate depends on how strenuous the activity is. The heart is able to pump more blood more quickly around the circulatory system. As more blood returns to the heart the cardiac muscle is stretched more than usual and this stimulates SAN to increase heart rate and it also increases the force of contraction, this is referred to as Starling's Law.

Blood flow is directed to the working muscles, heart and brain since they need more oxygen, whereas other areas of the body (the stomach and gut for example) do not require the oxygen as urgently. This process is known as vascular shunting. Blood distribution is also aided by precapillary sphincters, rings of muscle that surround blood vessels at the junction between an arteriole and capillary. It can effectively open and close the capillary and facilitates shunting.

The jargon

Mitochondria is the power house of the cell where the krebs cycle and electron transport system generates adenosine triphosphate (ATP).

Checkpoint 4

Describe the type of activities that should be included in a cool-down for a sport of your choice.

Grade booster

Be able to link the effects of warming up on the body to the benefits for performance.

Exam practice

answers: page 29

The heart plays an essential role in allowing the body to take part in a wide range of physical activity.

1 Explain the short-term effect that exercise has on stroke volume, cardiac output and heart rate. (6 minutes)
2 Describe the effect that physical exercise has on blood flow, blood velocity and blood pressure, accounting for any changes. (7 minutes)

The respiratory system

The human body needs a constant supply of oxygen. This oxygen is used to break down food to release energy. The body takes in oxygen continually from the air, as well as expelling carbon dioxide, a by-product from the breakdown of food into energy. This process of exchanging gases within the lungs is known as respiration.

The lungs

In order to get oxygen into our circulatory system, we first need to inhale air. This air ends up in our lungs, two spongy elastic bags in the airtight thoracic cavity, which extract oxygen from the inhaled air. Air is drawn into the lungs via the trachea. The lungs consist of a branching network of tubes called bronchioles (see diagram below). The bronchioles end in small sacs called alveoli and it is here that gaseous exchange takes place.

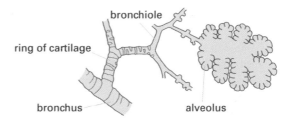

bronchiole

ring of cartilage

bronchus

alveolus

Checkpoint 1

How is the trachea protected against closure?

When we are resting, breathing is a process that occurs automatically. As we inhale, the only muscle that contracts is the diaphragm. This dome-shaped muscle flattens, increasing the volume of the thoracic cavity and causing air to rush into the lungs. As the diaphragm relaxes, it returns to its original shape, reducing the volume of the thoracic cavity and forcing air out of the lungs.

During exercise the demand for oxygen grows and we need to use extra muscles to help us breathe. The external intercostals aid inhalation, the internal intercostals aid exhalation.

Checkpoint 2

State two effects on breathing when taking exercise.

Respiration at rest

When we breathe at rest, we inhale and exhale between 12 and 16 times a minute. This is known as our respiratory rate. Each time we breathe, about 500ml of air is moved. This is called our tidal volume and it can be measured using a spirometer. The amount of air we breathe in one minute is known as minute ventilation and can be calculated by multiplying tidal volume and respiratory rate. Even after maximum expiration, about 1.5 litres of air remains in the lungs. This is called the residual volume.

Checkpoint 3

What does a spirometer measure?

The jargon

Tidal volume is the amount of air moved each time we breathe, usually about 500ml.

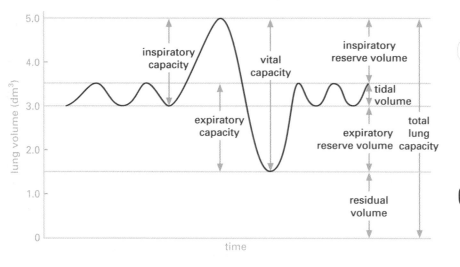

Action point

Study the graph and state the volumes of gas exchanged for each of the terms.

Examiner's secrets

Lung volumes is a popular focus for questions. Take a calculator to the exam in case you have to work out volumes.

Gaseous exchange

In the alveoli there is a thin film of moisture in which the oxygen dissolves and then diffuses into blood capillaries. Carbon dioxide diffuses from the blood into the alveoli (see diagram below).

Checkpoint 4

What happens to residual volume during physical activity?

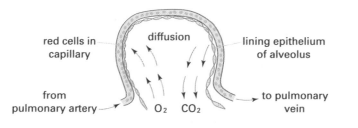

Control of breathing

Breathing is controlled by a respiratory centre found within the medulla oblongata. The centre is sensitive to pH levels in the blood and also receives information from chemoreceptors around the body that can detect changes in pH levels, which is an indicator of changing carbon dioxide concentration.

Exam practice   answers: page 29

1 Describe the pathway taken by air travelling from the nostrils to the blood capillaries in the left lung.   (8 minutes)
2 How are the terminal structures of the lungs specialised for the process of gaseous exchange?   (6 minutes)

Nutrition and sport

The food we eat and the liquids we drink help to keep us alive and functioning properly. In terms of sport, they also provide us with fuel for energy. The food we eat is broken down by the body's digestive system into different nutrients. It is these nutrients that provide us with energy and also help to keep the body functioning efficiently. In order to remain fit and healthy, the human body needs 46 nutrients. These can all be found in the seven major food groups that we eat:

→ carbohydrates
→ fats
→ proteins
→ water
→ vitamins
→ minerals
→ fibre.

A balanced diet

There are seven classes of food and each plays an important role in the diet of sports performers. Depending on the needs of their sport, performers will need to manipulate the food they eat to match both their energy and nutrient demands. For the vast majority of sports people, carbohydrates remain the most important element of their diet.

Food type	Role in sport
Carbohydrates (CHO)	The key energy source. Sports performers should eat a diet that is at least 70% CHO. Performers will also manipulate their intake of CHO according to their Glycemic Index (see page 24).
Fats	Also used as an energy source – especially in endurance and sub-maximal sports activities. Performers' diets should be made up of 18–24% fat – though this should be mainly unsaturated fat.
Fibre	Its main role is aiding digestion and ensuring that performers get the majority of the nutrients out of the food they eat.
Minerals	Required to maintain health, growth and development. Minerals are essential for the majority of metabolic and physiological processes that create movement in the human body.
Proteins	Can be used as a fuel source though its main role in sport is to facilitate building, repair and replacement of body tissue, especially muscle. Sports performers should eat a diet made up of 15% protein.

Vitamins	Essential to maintain good health and normal growth and development. Vitamins also aid many of the body's chemical reactions, especially those that are involved in growth and repair. Many sports performers take vitamin supplements to ensure this role is at its optimum.
Water	Keeps the body hydrated, which helps the body to regulate temperature and also transport nutrients and fuel to the working tissues.

Hydration and dehydration

To avoid dehydration it is vital to replace fluid regularly. During normal day-to-day activity, we lose fluid from our body constantly through the air we exhale and in our sweat. During sport, we lose even more. It is estimated that a marathon runner can lose up to 5 litres of fluid during a race. There are three main guidelines to avoiding dehydration:

→ Be fully hydrated before competition
→ Take fluids regularly throughout the activity – little and often is the mantra
→ Replace lost fluid as quickly as possible after playing.

Checkpoint 1

How can athletes maintain their hydration levels?

Take note

Drinking too much fluid can have a negative effect on sports performance.

Food and energy balance

The CHO and fats we eat are converted to energy and used when we take part in sport and physical activity. Energy is measured in kilojoules (Kj). On average, we need between 9,000 and 12,000 Kj (2,200–2,800Kcal) per day, but sports performers who are training and competing will often need double these figures.

In order to control our body weight, there is a simple formula that must be considered:

Energy intake = Energy expenditue

This is usually referred to as the energy balance. If energy intake is greater than energy expenditure then we will gain weight and vice versa. This is also linked to the basic metabolic rate (MR) – the minimal level of energy that is needed by the body, which varies from person to person. Generally, MR is high during our teenage years but slows down as we get older. If we do not reduce our food intake or increase our energy expenditure, the result will be a gain in weight. This is often referred to as creeping obesity or middle-age spread.

Eating before, during and after competition

Most sports performers use a strategy called carbo loading in both their training and preparation for competition. Carbo loading refers to eating a diet high in CHO, which should ensure that muscle glycogen stores are topped up before competition. Normally, performers will move towards low fibre or liquid foods the closer they get to competition. This should ensure that they will not be affected by gastrointestinal problems during competition and that the nutrients from the pre-match food are easily digested and utilised.

Glycemic Index

The Glycemic Index (also glycaemic index) or GI is a ranking system for carbohydrates based on their effect on blood glucose levels. It compares the available carbohydrate gram for gram of individual foods. Carbohydrates that break down rapidly have a high GI rating, cause a rapid rise in blood glucose levels and are very suitable for recovery after exercise. Carbohydrates that break down slowly have a low GI rating and are more often used before performance.

The research on sport and GI suggests that the best foods to eat in the last few hours before sport are carbohydrates with a low GI index. Though this may depend on the sport played, if the activity lasts more than an hour then continuing to eat CHO in the pre-match phase is very important. However, if the sports activity involves working at over 50 per cent VO_2 max then a CHO with a high GI rating that can be ingested easily, for example, a sports drink or gel bar should be used.

All athletes need to be aware that eating too much CHO before sport can lead to a 'hypoglycemic backlash'. The CHO-rich food and drink triggers the liver into converting too much of the resultant glucose into stored glycogen – but the physical activity will quickly use up the blood glucose and there will then be a 'hollow' period during which the body has to wait for the glycogen to be converted into glucose.

Classification	GI range	Food examples
Low GI	55 or less	Most fruit and veg, beans, wholegrains, all bran, brown bread
Medium GI	56–59	Croissants, raisins, pineapples
High GI	60 or above	Potatoes, cornflakes, doughnuts, baked potatoes, white bread

Eating after sport

During most sporting activity, performers will lose a lot of muscle glycogen, a small amount of body fat, some protein and lots of fluids. Research by the Australian Institute of Sport identified that the key strategy is to eat within two hours of training or competition and that the diet should include a high percentage of CHO moderate protein and plenty of fluids. Many élite performers now use liquid foods such as commercially made high-CHO drinks or homemade fruit smoothies, which are easy to digest and allow the speedy intake of the nutrients that assist recovery.

For the quickest replacement of glycogen, performers need to eat 1–2g of CH per kilogram of body weight in the two hours after sport. Muscle glycogen can generally be replaced at 5 per cent per hour, so it takes about 20 hours to refill an empty glycogen fuel tank after strenuous training or competition.

Protein provides the body with the amino acids necessary to rebuild muscle tissue damaged during sport. Protein can also increase the absorption of water from the intestines and improve muscle hydration. Protein shakes and drinks are easier to digest after exercise.

Fitness training and testing

Physical fitness is the ability of the body to meet the demands placed upon it. The level of fitness of a sports performer has a major effect on their performance.

Fitness

Fitness in sport is generally based around two groups of components.

Health-related fitness
→ Cardiovascular endurance
→ Muscular strength
→ Muscular endurance
→ Flexibility
→ Body composition

Skill-related fitness
→ Agility
→ Balance
→ Coordination
→ Power
→ Reaction time
→ Speed

Developing your physical fitness is one way of developing a healthy lifestyle, but it is important to recognise that there other components that contribute to the maintenance of a healthy lifestyle:

→ Exercise
→ Hygiene
→ Diet
→ Rest

Principles of training

In order to reap the full benefits of exercise, you need to train in a specific way. The aim of training is to improve the level of fitness, but this will only occur if you overload the body. Overloading the body will mean that gradually the body adapts to the new level of work. To ensure that overload is achieved, performers use the FITT principles:

→ F is for **Frequency** – the number of times you train a week. To achieve overload, this needs to be regular.
→ I is for **Intensity** – how had you work. To achieve overload, the level of intensity will need to be gradually increased.
→ T is for **Time** – how long you train. Increasing the duration of exercise increases the overload on your body.
→ T is for **Type** – some training is very specific to certain kinds of sport.

In order that training is both safe and effective, the training programme needs to be planned carefully. Applying the five main principles of training (**SPORT**) should ensure this:

→ Specificity – choose the right training for the sport and also the position/role played. Training should be planned so that the performer's body systems adapt to the specific demands of the sport.
→ Progression – gradually increase the trworkload as you train.
→ Overload – make the body work harder so that the required physiological adaptations occur.
→ Reversibility – understand that fitness cannot be stored for future use and will disappear if you stop training.
→ Tedium – keep varying the training in order to maintain motivation.

Thresholds and intensity of training

Involves calculating work intensities for optimal gains from training. The most common strategies used by athletes are monitoring heart rate and the **Borg Scale**. A common method of calculating a desired fitness training zone is by using the **Karvonen Formula**.

This is calculated as follows:

→ 220 – age of performer = maximum heart rate (MHR)
→ MHR – resting heart rate = heart rate reserve
→ heart rate reserve x training zone + resting heart rate = training heart rate

The different heart rate zones include:

Recovery zone	60–70%	
Aerobic zone	70–80%	Exercising in this zone will help to develop your aerobic system
Anaerobic zone	80–90%	Training in this zone will help to increase your lactate threshold and improve the body's ability to cope with lactic acid.

Fitness testing

Reasons for testing

Fitness testing is used to help performers identify their training needs and check on progression. The tests are specific to the different fitness components and increasingly there are also sport-specific fitness tests. By repeating fitness tests after completing a training programme and comparing them with tests carried out earlier, it is possible to see how fitness levels have improved.

A performer's physical and skill fitness can be measured using a series of tests. The key is to select the tests that specifically measure the components required in the performer's sport and or position. Motor fitness tests look at the neuromuscular components of fitness and are linked to skill–fitness components. Physical fitness tests focus on the anatomical and physiological components that influence a performer's physical performance capacity

Principle of maximal and sub-maximal tests

Fitness tests can be maximal or sub maximal. Maximal tests require the performer to work progressively harder until maximal effort occurs (the multi-stage fitness test is a good example of a maximal test). Sub-maximal tests may still be progressive but the performer will not reach maximal effort. These tests often use heart-rate response to exercise in order to track the level of exercise (the Harvard step test is an example of a sub-maximal test).

Fitness tests

Testing for	Common tests used in sport
Strength	Hand-grip dynamometer One maximal lift
Speed	30m sprint
Power	Standing broad jump Vertical (sargeant) jump
Local muscular endurance	Abdominal conditioning test
Cardiovascular endurance	Multi-stage fitness test
Flexibility	Sit and reach test
Agility	Illinois agility run

You will need to give the basic protocol for each test. This simply requires you to describe how the test is undertaken.

Training methods

Training method	Description	Fitness component
Continuous	Also known as aerobic training. Sub-maximal training of at least 12 minutes in duration.	Cardiovascular endurance
Intermittent	Often referred to as interval training. Periods of exercise are followed by short periods of rest. This training method can be modified to develop both aerobic and anaerobic systems.	Cardiovascular endurance Muscular endurance
Circuit	Involves moving from one exercise to another, usually in a series of different stations or pieces of equipment. Work for a short duration at near maximal intensity can be modified to allow longer duration and lower intensity.	Muscular endurance Power Muscular strength
Weight	Involves working against a resistance, using repetitions and sets. Can be modified for anaerobic strength (few reps: heavy resistance/weights) or muscular endurance (many reps: light weights).	Muscular strength Power
Plyometrics	Involves combinations of actions such as hopping, skipping and bounding. Short duration, done in sets.	Power Speed
Mobility	Involves dynamic mobility exercise in a series of drills that take the body through the full range of movement in a controlled, dynamic way.	Flexibility Coordination

Answers
Anatomy and physiology

The skeletal and muscular system

Checkpoints

1 The human skeleton:
    1 provides **shape**
    2 supports the body in the correct **posture**
    3 **supports** the internal organs
    4 **protects** the body
    5 provides sites of **muscle attachment**
    6 creates **levers**
    7 enables us to make **movements**
    8 **produces** blood cells.
2 Synovial joints have a fluid sac that lubricates the joints. The bones do not actually articulate, allowing a range of movement. The ends of the bones are covered with cartilage which acts as a shock absorber.
3 Ligaments attach bone to bone and prevent unwanted movement; tendons attach muscle to bone and act as a pulley.
4 The epimysium's role is to protect the muscle and help it slide smoothly past nearby muscles, bones and other organs as it changes in length.

Exam practice

The functions of the skeleton facilitate physical activity by:
*   providing shape for the body
*   supporting the body in the correct posture
*   supporting and protecting vital organs during movement
*   providing a site for muscle attachment
*   working as a lever system
*   storing calcium, nutrients and minerals needed to repair the body after strenuous activity.

Motion and movement

Checkpoints

1 The structures that make up the body's nervous system are the brain, spinal cord, nerve fibre and effector and receptor organs.
2 The all-or-none law states that all the fibres in a single motor unit receive the same neural stimulation, so they all act maximally when the threshold of stimulation is met.
3 The neurone and muscle fibres it stimulates make up what is called the motor unit.
4 Effector organs receive information and instructions from the brain. Receptor organs transmit information to the brain.

Exam practice

Type 1 – slow oxidative fibres – endurance activities such as middle- and long-distance running, swimming and cycling.

Type 11a – Fast oxidative glycolytic fibres (FOG) – fast anaerobic activities such as sprinting.

Type 11b – Fast glycolytic fibres (FG) – speed and power, in short bursts, for example in weightlifting.

Laws of motion

Checkpoints

1 A vector quality possesses both magnitude and direction. A scalar quality is described completely in terms of its magnitude.
2 Acceleration is calculated as the change in velocity divided by the time taken to change.
3 The correct units of measurement for speed, velocity and acceleration are: speed – ms^{-1}, velocity – ms^{-1} and acceleration – ms^{-2}.
4 A horizontal line on a distance v time graph represents stationary.

Exam practice

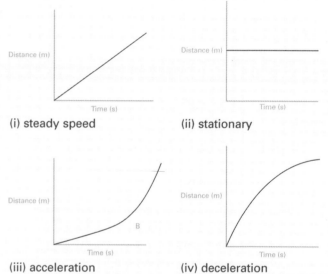

(i) steady speed

(ii) stationary

(iii) acceleration

(iv) deceleration

The cardiovascular system

Checkpoints

1 The left ventricle is thicker walled than the right ventricle because the left ventricle pumps blood around the whole body, whereas the right ventricle only pumps blood from the heart to the lungs.
2 Stimulation of the parasympathetic system slows down the heart beat.
3 Stimulation of the sympathetic system speeds up the heart beat.

Exam practice

Venous return is the volume of blood returned to the right atrium. It is aided by exercise in that the muscle pump action forces more blood back to the heart. Exercise will also cause hypertrophy of the heart, creating a more forceful pump.

The role of blood in transporting oxygen and carbon dioxide

Checkpoints

1 Myoglobin transports oxygen within the muscles because it has a greater affinity with oxygen than haemoglobin.
2 Oxygen, via the blood, enters the blood network via the alveoli within the lungs.
3 Vasodilation is the increase in the diameter of a blood vessel, resulting from the relaxation of the surrounding muscles. This causes an increase in blood flow.
4 A cool-down should include light continuous exercise that maintains a higher than normal heart rate and also stretching.

Exam practice

1 Short-term effect of exercise on:

stroke volume – increases

heart rate – increases

cardiac output – increases
2 Effects of physical exercise on:

blood flow – increases due to the increased needs of the muscles; shunting means blood is moved away from some areas; muscles need lots of blood and oxygen

blood velocity – increases, since the heart needs to pump harder and faster; may depend on type of blood vessel

blood pressure – increases due to increased heart rate; many blood vessels may also undergo vasoconstriction which also increases pressure.

The respiratory system

Checkpoints

1 The trachea is protected against closure by rings of cartilage.
2 When taking exercise, there is an increase in the depth and frequency of breathing.
3 A spirometer records the depth and frequency of breathing and can be used to study oxygen consumption.
4 Residual volume stays the same during physical activity.

Exam practice

1 The pathway of air when travelling from the nostrils to the blood capillaries in the left lung is as follows: pharynx → larynx → trachea → left bronchus → left bronchiole → alveolus.
2 The terminal structures of the lungs are specialised for the process of gaseous exchange by: vast surface area, very thin walled/one cell thick, elastic tissue, moist membrane, extensive surrounding blood supply, extensive capillary network.

Nutrition and sport

Checkpoints

1 The two energy-producing components in the diet are carbohydrate and fat.
2 An athlete's diet should be made up of about 15 per cent protein.
3 Keeps the body hydrated which helps the body to regulate temperature and also transport nutrients and fuel to the working tissues.

Exam practice

The main guidelines to avoiding dehydration should include:
1 Be fully hydrated before competition.
2 Take fluids regularly throughout the activity – little and often is the mantra.
3 Replace lost fluid as quickly as possible after playing.

Fitness training and testing

Checkpoints

1 The components that contribute to the maintenance of a healthy lifestyle includes exercise, diet, hygiene and rest.
2 Fitness testing is used to help performers identify their training needs and check on progression.
3 Continuous training consists of sub-maximal training of at least 12 minutes in duration, which develops cardiovascular endurance.

Exam practice

Specificity	Choosing training methods that are appropriate to your sport or position.
Progression	Setting achievable targets/increasing training volume.
Overload	Stressing the body above that which it has become accustomed to.
Reversibility or regression	If the training load is not maintained then the athlete's level of fitness will begin to revert back to that of pre-training.
Tedium or variance	Using different methods of training to prevent mental and physical plateaus.

Revision checklist
Anatomy and physiology

By the end of this chapter you should be able to:

1	Describe the structure and function of the skeletal system.	Confident	Not confident **Revise** pages 10–11
2	Describe and discuss the types of movement that can occur in the main synovial joints of the body	Confident	Not confident **Revise** pages 10–11
3	Give an overview of the structure of muscles and their role in creating movement.	Confident	Not confident **Revise** pages 10–13
4	Describe how skeletal muscle is divided into three main fibre types	Confident	Not confident **Revise** pages 11–13
5	Explain how the muscular system allows us to maintain our body position and move body parts.	Confident	Not confident **Revise** pages 11–13
6	Understand how the body's nervous system enables us to coordinate and control our movements.	Confident	Not confident **Revise** pages 11–13
7	Discuss the definitions and laws of motion.	Confident	Not confident **Revise** pages 14–15
8	Outline the different types of motion that occur in sport.	Confident	Not confident **Revise** pages 14–15
9	Explain the difference between scalar and vector quantities.	Confident	Not confident **Revise** pages 14–15
10	Describe the structure and function of the heart.	Confident	Not confident **Revise** pages 16–17
11	Understand how blood supply is controlled.	Confident	Not confident **Revise** pages 16–17
12	Describe how oxygen is transported around the body.	Confident	Not confident **Revise** pages 16–17
13	Explain the effects of warming up and cooling down.	Confident	Not confident **Revise** pages 18–19
14	Understand the effects of exercise on blood.	Confident	Not confident **Revise** page 19
15	Describe the mechanics of respiration.	Confident	Not confident **Revise** pages 20–21
16	Understand how breathing is controlled by a respiratory centre in the brain.	Confident	Not confident **Revise** pages 20–21
17	Understand the role nutrition plays in the preparation for sporting activity.	Confident	Not confident **Revise** pages 22–24

Skill acquisition

Skill is defined as the learnt ability to bring about pre-determined results with maximum certainty with the minimum outlay of energy. Skilled performers show the consistent characteristics of efficiency, coordination, fluency and a high level of technique. We will revise the different types of skills, their characteristics and the varied continua used in an attempt to classify skills. Performing well in sport relies on inherited abilities and we will look at the key characteristics of ability. The way that we gather information, decide what needs to be done and then execute a response is referred to as information processing. Once learnt, skills are retained in the memory and we need to understand the memory process and also suggest strategies for improving our retention and retrieval of information. Performance in competition is affected by our motivation and level of arousal and this may depend on the stage of learning we are in. How we learn skills is also affected by the quality of guidance and demonstration we are given.

Exam themes

- Characteristics of skilled performance
- The classification of sports skills
- Skills, ability and information processing
- Information processing and memory
- Motor and executive programmes
- Memory and learning theories
- Motivation, guidance and improving performance
- The role of reinforcement and demonstration in the learning of skills
- Guidance and teaching styles

Topic checklist

	Edexcel	AQA		OCR		WJEC	
	Not examined	AS	A2	AS	A2	AS	A2
Characteristics and types of skills		○		○		○	
Memory		○		○		○	
Motivation			●	○			●
Feedback		○		○		○	

Characteristics and types of skills

Skill is the learnt ability to bring about pre-determined results with maximum efficiency, often with the minimum outlay of time or energy or both.

Knapp

Skilled performance is said to be:

→ intentional and consistent
→ goal directed
→ learnt – practice is required
→ high quality
→ minimum energy outlay
→ maximum efficiency.

Perceptual, cognitive and motor skills

→ **Perceptual skill** – complex definition – involves interpretation of stimuli – based on demands and past experiences.
→ **Cognitive skill** – skill in mental processes such as learning.
→ **Motor skill** – task that has a goal and requires body and/or limb movement.

Ability

Ability is seen as **innate** (genetically determined) and enduring, often enhanced by early childhood experience.

Ability allows us to complete various tasks, although there are actually two identified types of ability:

→ **Psychomotor ability** involves the *processing* of information and the *initiation* of movement.
→ **Gross motor ability** involves *actual movement* of the body.

Checkpoint 1

Explain the main difference between a skill and an ability.

Classifying movement skills

This is where we place and justify movement skills on a variety of continua, the most common of which are:

→ **Muscular involvement** which ranges from gross (large) to fine (delicate).
→ **Environmental influence** which ranges from open (unpredictable and changing) to closed (stable and predictable).
→ **Continuity** which ranges from discrete (definite start and end), serial (linked series of sub routines) and continuous (no clear beginning or end).
→ **Pacing** ranging from externally paced to internally paced.
→ **Difficulty** ranging from simple to complex.
→ **Organisation** ranging from low to high.

Checkpoint 2

Why do we try to classify skills?

Information processing

This is the process by which the sports performer gathers information, decides what action is required and then reacts accordingly. In sport this all has to happen in a split second (see diagram).

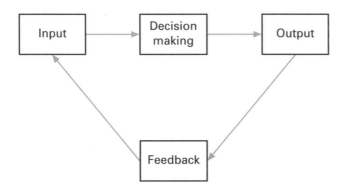

Feedback is received from both internal and external sources and means that the performer can make adjustments if the same situation arises again.

Schmidt identified three basic phases to information processing:

→ **Stage 1 stimulus identification**   Here the sense organs of the body pick up information from the environment by looking for cues.
→ **Stage 2 response selection**   Once all the information has been received a decision is made.
→ **Stage 3 response programming**   The decision taken sets in motion an appropriate response. This will often be a motor programme.

Motor programmes

Also referred to as '**executive programmes**', motor programmes are stored movement patterns held in the long-term memory that can be retrieved when a certain stimulus is received.

The speed that we process this information and elicit a response is known as **reaction time**. The time between starting and finishing the movement is called **movement time**. The time between the stimulus being identified and the completion of the movement is referred to as the **response time** and can also be calculated by using reaction time plus movement time.

There are several factors that affect these times:

→ Whether the reaction requires choice.
→ Age and sex of performer.
→ Whether the performer is expecting a stimulus also known as stimulus-response compatibility.
→ Previous experience.
→ How quickly one response follows the other, known as the psychological refractory period.
→ Anticipation of what is going to happen.

The single-channel hypothesis states that we can only deal with one stimulus at a time. This is how sports performers can 'sell a dummy' – if we can get our opponent to wrongly anticipate our action, it takes too long for them to change their decision if we then alter our move.

Examiner's secrets

Other versions of the diagram may be given in the exam paper. Don't worry – just work through each stage, looking for the three basics phases.

Grade booster

Be able to apply the phases of information processing to a range of sports skills.

Checkpoint 3

Describe the three phases of the information-processing model.

Grade booster

A theory linked to the psychological refractory period is the single-channel hypothesis and this is often the focus for questions.

Checkpoint 4

Explain the link between 'selling a dummy' in sport and the single-channel hypothesis.

Exam practice   answers: page 40

Explain how a tennis serve contains both open and closed elements.

(6 minutes)

Memory

Memory plays a very important part in how performers process information. Previous experiences affect how we interpret the information we receive when playing sport. Often, our previous experiences in sport can affect how we judge and interpret information when we perform.

Types of memory

Memory is a complex concept, although the basic aspects can be summarised in the following diagram:

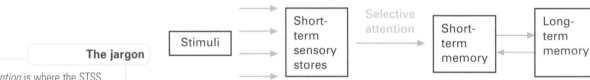

Short-term sensory store (STSS) – large capacity but can only hold information for up to one second, acts as a filter leading to selective attention.

Short-term memory (STM) – often referred to as the 'working memory', decides what needs to be done, limited capacity 7+/–2 items for about 30 seconds, information that is considered important or that can be rehearsed is passed on to the long-term memory store.

Long-term memory (LTM) – limitless capacity and can hold information for long periods of time. Memory that passes into the LTM will have been encoded (chunked or associated); motor programmes are stored in the LTM since they can be rehearsed.

Strategies to help improve information retention and retrieval include chunking, repetition or rehearsal and association.

Learning theories

There are two main schools of thought.

Associationist/connectionist	Cognitive
Stimulus – Response S–R	Intervening variables
Conditioned by stimuli – connected to response	Thinking leading to insight learning
Classical – Pavlov – conditioned reflex	Insight is facilitated by past experiences
Operant – Skinner – trial and error	Gestaltists – whole (Koffka, Koehler)
Drive theory – Hull	Leads to whole practice

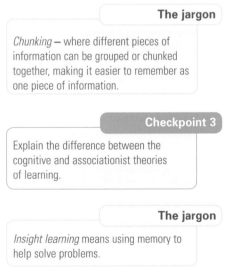

The jargon

Selective attention is where the STSS sorts out relevant and irrelevant information, allowing the sports performer to concentrate on the important information and shut out any distractions.

Checkpoint 1

Describe the three types of memory we use.

Checkpoint 2

Explain how the strategy of chunking helps us to retain and retrieve information.

The jargon

Chunking – where different pieces of information can be grouped or chunked together, making it easier to remember as one piece of information.

Checkpoint 3

Explain the difference between the cognitive and associationist theories of learning.

The jargon

Insight learning means using memory to help solve problems.

Phases of learning

Fitts and Possner identified three phases of learning:

Phase	Description
Cognitive phase	Beginners' phase, lots of trial and error, lots of positive feedback required.
Associative phase	Motor or intermediate phase, associates movement with mental image, motor programme developing.
Autonomous phase	Automatic, little conscious thought, distractions ignored, motor programmes now in LTM.

Checkpoint 4

Which of Fitts and Possner's phases of learning do we usually associate with beginners?

Grade booster

You need to know the characteristics for each of the phases of learning and be able to give practical examples of how this knowledge would be used in improving a performer's skill level.

Transfer

Transfer refers to the influence of the learning or performance of one skill on the learning or performance of another. There are a number of different types of transfer we investigate in sports:

Type of transfer	Description
Positive	Where a skill can help with the learning of another.
Negative	Where a skill hinders the learning of another.
Proactive	Influences a skill yet to be learnt.
Retroactive	Influences the performance of a previously learnt skill.
Bilateral	Transfer of skill learnt on one side of body to the other side.

Schmidt's schema theory is similar to the theory of transfer. Skills learnt in one sport can be used in others as the performer has developed a general set of motor programmes that helps skills to be adapted to suit the sporting situation. This also solves the problem of having to store millions of separate motor programmes for every conceivable sporting movement.

Action point

Give a practical example from sport for each of the types of transfer highlighted in the table.

The jargon

A *schema* is a mental framework or outline developed through past experience.

Exam practice   answers: page 40

Schmidt introduced the concept of 'schema theory'. Using the practical example of a basketball shot, explain the components of this theory.

(6 minutes)

Motivation

To be able to perform at our best in sport, we have to *want* to perform well and achieve. This drive to do well is referred to as motivation. The job of the coach or captain in sport is to motivate their teams to perform at their very best.

Types of motivation in sport

Motivation is the need and desire to perform at our best. There are two main factors that can affect motivation: extrinsic and intrinsic.

Intrinsic motivation	Extrinsic motivation
Internal drive to perform well	Rewards such as medals, money, prizes
Positive emotions	Significant others may also motivate
Martens – mastery of task and self-achievement	Rewards act as reinforcers

The jargon

Motivation is the internal mechanisms and external stimuli which arouse and direct our behaviour.

The jargon

Significant other is a person who a performer relates to and holds in high esteem.

Checkpoint 1

Explain the difference between intrinsic and extrinsic motivation.

Demonstration and presentation of skills

→ Demonstrations are very important in learning sports skills and this links to the theories of observational learning and guidance.
→ Practice sessions should include activities that allow for the maximum amount of transfer to take place.

Part practice and whole practice

The teaching of skills in practice sessions often varies depending on the skills being taught. Complex routines in sports like gymnastics are best taught by breaking them up into smaller parts called sub routines. This type of practice is called part practice.

Where the skill is more dynamic or continuous, such as a golf swing or a tennis serve, it is better to teach the whole skill to allow the learner to get the true feel for the skill. This is called whole practice.

Other methods of teaching include progressive part where the learner learns one part of the skill before moving on to learn the next sub routine, this is often referred to as 'linking'.

The whole-part-whole method is a combination of the whole and part methods. The whole skill is taught first to give the learner experience of the whole skill and it is broken down to refine the individual sub routines.

Links

Check out how motivation is linked to arousal levels in the sports psychology section, see page 81.

Checkpoint 2

What type of sports skills is best taught using the part practice model?

The concept of transfer

Transfer refers to the influence of the learning or performance of one skill on the learning or performance of another. This influence can be positive where it helps the new skill or it can be negative where it hinders the learning or performance of the other skill.

Proactive transfer is where the influence is on a skill yet to be learnt, whereas retroactive transfer is where the influence is on the performance of a previously learnt skill.

There are three main types of **guidance** that are used in teaching skills in sport:

Type of guidance	Description
Visual	Showing what needs to be done either by demonstration or using video
Verbal	Telling the performer what needs to be done
Physical	Manually or mechanically assisting the performer to carry out the task

Teaching styles

Mosston and Ashworth identified a variety of teaching styles:

Teaching style	Description
Command	Teacher makes all the decisions
Reciprocal	Learners work in pairs and become teachers
Discovery	Decisions made by learner with guidance/ input from teacher
Problem solving	Learner makes all the decisions

Successful teachers and coaches tend to adopt a range of the above styles depending on the conditions and in order to respond to the needs of their pupils.

The jargon

Physical guidance helps to develop *kinaesthetic awareness*. This is where the performer has an awareness of body and limb position during movement.

Checkpoint 3

Give an example where manual guidance can help a performer cope with fear.

Checkpoint 4

What variables should be taken into account when choosing a teaching style?

Grade booster

You will need to be able to justify the effective use and limitation for each style of teaching.

Exam practice answers: page 40

Motivation is a key element in preparing for a sports performance.

1 Explain the term 'intrinsic motivation'. (4 minutes)

2 What external pressures can affect the motivation of a performer preparing for a high-level sports competition? (8 minutes)

Feedback

Feedback is the process which tells us how we are getting on while we perform a skill and afterwards can tell us how well we did. Feedback also completes the loop of the information-processing system, becoming part of the input and so affecting the performer's next decision (see diagram).

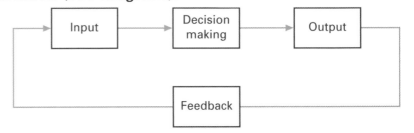

Types of feedback

There are several forms of feedback:

Type	Description
Continuous feedback	Feedback during the performance, often in the form of kinaesthesis
Terminal feedback	Feedback after the skill has been executed
Knowledge of results	A type of terminal feedback that gives the performer information about the end result
Knowledge of performance	Information on how well the skill or movement is being performed
Internal or intrinsic feedback	A type of continuous feedback that reports how we feel, called proprioception
External or extrinsic feedback	Feedback that comes from an external source such as a coach
Positive feedback	Feedback that reinforces the learning or performance of a skill or gives information about a successful outcome
Negative feedback	Feedback on an unsuccessful result, can be used to prepare for future performance

The jargon

Proprioception is the awareness of the shape and position of the body, an internal form of feedback.

In practice, feedback in sport is usually divided into two methods: knowledge of performance and knowledge of results. Both types can be used to help motivate a performer, however, if used incorrectly they can hinder future performance.

Checkpoint 1

Explain the difference between external feedback and internal feedback.

Knowledge of performance

Knowledge of performance tells performers how well or badly they are performing/executing a skill. Some of this feedback comes from proprioception – our own body awareness (you can feel how hard you have struck a ball in football or hit the ball in a golf shot). Knowledge of performance can also be given as an external source of feedback from a coach or peer – they can give verbal feedback on your performance.

Videoing particular elements of a performance and then analysing the execution of a skill can also be an effective form of this feedback.

Knowledge of results

Knowledge of results gives performers feedback on the outcome of their actions. Once again, it can come from a number of different sources. In some sports, such as gymnastics, proprioception can give the performers feedback on the outcome – they can feel that they have landed badly. Most, though, comes from external sources – a coach or teacher commenting on the performance. It is extremely important for performers to know what the results of their action have been. There can be very little learning without knowledge of results, especially in the early stages of learning a skill.

Both of these types of feedback play an important role in the concept of reinforcement. If a performance has been successful, either in terms of executing the skill or the result is good, then the performer will feel satisfied and the Stimulus–Response (S–R) bond is strengthened. Also, understanding and feeling that the movement and result is good will help the performer form a picture of what is correct and to associate future performance with that model.

Checkpoint 2

Explain the difference between knowledge of results and knowledge of performance.

Checkpoint 3

Explain the relationship between feedback and reinforcement.

The importance of feedback when learning a new skill

→ Positive feedback that encourages learners will motivate them to try harder.
→ Being told a performance was good by an external source helps to reinforce the skill in the performer's mind.
→ Feedback that gives suggestions on how to improve performance should result in more skilful movement.

The principles of feedback

The type of feedback given should depend on a number of factors:
→ The ability of the performer.
→ The type of activity being undertaken.
→ The personality of the performer.

Feedback needs to be given as soon as possible after the performance, the longer the delay between performance and feedback the less effective the feedback will be. The aim is to get the performers to associate the feeling of the skill with a positive result.

Any feedback given needs to be clear, concise and easily understood.

Examiner's secrets

You will often be asked to give practical examples in your answer to questions on feedback. Try to note down examples from your own sport where the various types of feedback could be used.

Checkpoint 4

What should a coach take into consideration before deciding on the type of feedback to use with a performer?

Exam practice   answers: pages 40–41

Feedback involves using information that is available to a performer during and after the execution of a skill.

1 Outline the different types of feedback that can be used to help performers improve their performance.   (8 minutes)

2 What factors should a coach take into consideration before using feedback to help a performer improve?   (6 minutes)

Answers
Skill acquisition

Characteristics and types of skills

Checkpoints

1 The difference between a skill and an ability in that a skill is learnt and an ability is innate.

2 There are many different skills linked to such a variety of sporting activities that classification is an attempt to simplify the study of skills.

3 The three basic phases of information processing are:
   Stage 1   stimulus identification
   Stage 2   response selection
   Stage 3   response programming.

4 The single-channel hypothesis states that we can only deal with one stimulus at a time. This is how sports performers can 'sell a dummy' – if we can get our opponent to wrongly anticipate our action it takes too long for them to change their decision if we then alter our move.

Exam practice

A tennis serve contains both open and closed skills.

Closed – isolated skill, not greatly affected by environment, movement replication always the same.

Open – factors such as heat and humidity can affect ball flight, server may perceive some movement of opponent and respond by changing their own movement, player can vary the type of serve.

Memory

Checkpoints

1 The three types of memory are:

   Short-term sensory store – large capacity but can only hold information for up to one second, acts as a filter leading to selective attention.

   Short-term memory – often referred to as the 'working memory', decides what needs to be done, limited capacity 7+/–2 items for about 30 seconds.

   Long-term memory – limitless capacity and can hold information for long periods of time.

2 The strategy of chunking helps us to retain and retrieve information by grouping units of information together into short phrases.

3 Cognitive theories of learning suggest we need to understand a problem and that learning is facilitated by past experiences and we then select an appropriate response. Associationist theories of learning suggest that we learn a specific response to a specific stimulus.

4 Beginners are usually associated with Fitts and Possner's cognitive phase.

Exam practice

Experienced basketball player will have stored a program for the shot in their LTM. Recall scheme will start off the programme when the player wants to shoot. Adjustments may be made depending on external factors, after shot recognition schema – did it feel right, response outcome – was it successful?

Motivation

Checkpoints

1 Intrinsic motivation is an internal drive to perform well; extrinsic motivation includes rewards such as medals, money or prizes.

2 Complex routines in sports like gymnastics are best taught by breaking them up into smaller parts called sub routines.

3 An example of where manual guidance can help a performer cope with fear is by wearing arm bands in swimming.

4 Variables include the type and difficulty of the activity, the ability levels of the learners, the group's level of motivation, the age of the learners and the environmental conditions.

Exam practice

1 Intrinsic motivation comes from an internal feeling/ playing for its own sake, may include elements of fun, enjoyment and satisfaction, achieving a personal best or self-set goals. Would include achieving intrinsic rewards.

2 External pressures on a performer preparing for competition would include the following: external rewards that victory would bring, peer pressure from team, pressure from significant others (coach/ manager/parents), pressure from opponents or previous experience, the importance of the task, presence of a large audience or media, the conditions or environment of the scheduled playing time.

Feedback

Checkpoints

1 Internal feedback is a type of continuous feedback that reports how we feel, called proprioception, whereas external feedback is feedback that comes from an external source such as a coach.

2 Knowledge of results gives a performer feedback on the outcome of their actions. Knowledge of performance tells the performer how well or badly they are performing/executing a skill.

3 Feedback on a successful performance will mean that the performer will feel satisfied and the S–R bond is strengthened. They will be more likely to be successful the next time they perform.

4 A coach should consider the following factors before deciding on the type of feedback:
   • the ability of the performer
   • the type of activity being undertaken
   • the personality of the performer.

Exam practice

1 The different types of feedback that can be used to help performers improve their performance are:
Continuous feedback available during performance. Terminal feedback, knowledge of results available after performance. Knowledge of performance, could be internal or intrinsic or external feedback from a coach giving verbal or visual guidance. Positive feedback is used to reinforce learning.

2 Factors affecting the type of feedback used include the ability of the performer, what stage of learning they are in, the type and difficulty of activity, the personality of performer and the type of teaching style being used.

Grade booster

Try to back up the points you make in answers with a named theory or the name of a scientist who has carried out research in that specific area.

Examiner's secrets

Very often a diagram can help you explain a difficult concept such as information processing in a more efficient way.

Revision checklist
Skill aquisition

By the end of this chapter you should be able to:

1	Define the characteristics and types of skills.	Confident	Not confident **Revise** page 32
2	Explain the information-processing model.	Confident	Not confident **Revise** pages 32–33
3	Discuss the different types of memory and the role they play in learning and producing sports skills.	Confident	Not confident **Revise** pages 34–35
4	Understand the theory and the practical application of motor programmes.	Confident	Not confident **Revise** page 35
5	Describe the different types of motivation and their effects on sports performance.	Confident	Not confident **Revise** pages 36–37
6	Explain effective demonstration and presentation of skills to learners in sport.	Confident	Not confident **Revise** pages 36–37
7	Discuss the concept of transfer and its influence on the learning of skills.	Confident	Not confident **Revise** page 35
8	Discuss the three main types of guidance that are used in teaching skills in sport.	Confident	Not confident **Revise** page 37
9	Discuss how different teaching styles suit specific sporting situations.	Confident	Not confident **Revise** page 37
10	Explain the role feedback plays in the learning of skills.	Confident	Not confident **Revise** pages 38–39
11	Give examples of the various types of feedback.	Confident	Not confident **Revise** pages 38–39
12	Discuss and give practical applications of the principles of feedback.	Confident	Not confident **Revise** pages 38–39

The social contemporary study of sport

The contemporary issues unit investigates how society can affect the sports performer and how society can be influenced by physical education and sport. The terms we use when describing the activities related to sport are technical, which can lead to confusion, so we need to review the key concepts and terms used in the sociological study of sport. You need to be able to analyse these different terms in order to develop a better understanding of why people get involved in physical education and sport at different levels and the factors that influence and restrict their choices. In some of the exam specifications, this unit compares physical education and sport in the UK with that of other countries so that we can learn from the experiences of other cultures. Many social issues surround physical education and sport and we need to take an in-depth look at the main issues affecting the performer. Discrimination of all forms is unfortunately a feature of our society, in sport as in other aspects.

Exam themes

- The concepts of sport, leisure, play and recreation
- Physical and outdoor education in UK schools
- Sport within different cultures around the globe
- Sport in advanced cultures
- The support and nurture of élite sport
- Ethics and values in high-level sport
- The concept of mass participation
- Factors that affects a person's access to sport and recreation
- Issues in the Olympic Games

Topic checklist

	Edexcel		AQA		OCR		WJEC	
	AS	A2	AS	A2	AS	A2	AS	A2
Sport, leisure and recreation: key concepts	O		O		O		O	
Sport and culture					O			
Sport in advanced societies		●			O			●
Élite sport	O			●	O		O	
Ethics and values in high-level sport	O	●		●	O	●	O	
Sport and mass participation	O	●	O		O		O	●
Factors affecting participation	O		O		O		O	●
The Olympic Games	O		O		O		O	●
Issues at the Olympics	O		O		O			●
Sport, sponsorship and the media	O		O		O			

Sport, leisure and recreation: key concepts

The study of sports sociology identifies the effect society can have on the sports performer and also the effect sport may have on society. We first need to review the different terms used to describe the sociological aspects of sport and physical education.

The key concepts

Sports have the following characteristics:

→ they all contain an element of **chance**
→ they all involve **competition** between **distinct sides**
→ **physically strenuous activity** is involved
→ the **clear outcome** has **winners** and **losers**
→ games are **spontaneous** and **enjoyable**
→ **special equipment** is usually needed to play.

Leisure

Key words for leisure are: free time, choice, not work. Definitions of leisure tend to infer that it is time not at work, but work can include many things. Although there has always been some form of leisure throughout history, we all have more leisure time and can choose from a greater list of activities than people in the past.

Recreation

Physical recreation

Physical recreation is physical activity of a relaxing nature, with limited outcome and organisation. It is a positive use of leisure time, involving an activity worth doing. Physical recreation has a strong link with middle-class moral guidance of the nineteenth century. Intrinsic rewards dominate in physical recreation.

Outdoor recreation

Outdoor recreation involves challenging activities in the natural environment. Most people in Britain partake frequently in some form of outdoor recreation. For most people, the essential element is an escape from the urban environment. The most popular outdoor recreations are walking and fishing.

Play

Children play to increase their mastery of reality. Adults play to escape from reality. Because of its non-serious quality, a number of dimensions of play can be identified:

→ Play must be freely undertaken. If constrained, it is less playful.
→ Play is non-instrumental. It is an end in itself – you do not play for an outcome.

Take note

The key to leisure time is that you perform the activities that you *choose* to do.

Checkpoint 1

List four labour-saving devices that have enabled people who do housework to have more leisure time.

Checkpoint 2

Why, for professional sports performers, is a definition of leisure difficult?

Checkpoint 3

What factors have led to an increase in participation in outdoor sports?

→ Play generally has its own set of rules and regulations. It is very informal and any rules will be agreed by the participants and may well change during the activity.
→ Play activities involve uncertainty. Play is open-ended and has no limits.

Physical education

In the UK, physical education takes place only in educational institutions (schools, colleges and universities). It always involves a 'teacher' passing on knowledge to a group of 'pupils' and is almost always concerned with bodily movement. However, it is a wide concept with many different interpretations. Even with the National Curriculum for physical education, no one school's programme is the same as another's. In recent years, the academic study of physical education has grown greatly and it is now studied at many levels. The National Curriculum identifies six sport activity areas: games, athletics, gymnastics, dance, swimming and adventure. Schools should offer pupils experience in at least five of the activity areas.

Recent initiatives in physical education and school sport include TOP programmes, sports college status and the development of School Sport Partnership networks. The biggest impact has come from the PESSCL (PE, School Sport and Club Link) strategy as part of the whole sport plans to encourage the development of school club links and the linked development of School Sport Partnerships. School Sports Partnerships bring primary, special and secondary schools together in a network benefiting from extra staffing and funding to increase sports opportunities for pupils.

Outdoor education

Outdoor education forms some part of most school curricula and is now a stated aim of the National Curriculum. However, in most schools it is only an extracurricular activity. The problems are that outdoor pursuits are very expensive in terms of transport and equipment needed, and many safety precautions must be considered, especially in the light of several recent tragedies.

The jargon

The *National Curriculum* is issued by the government. It sets out what schools should teach pupils, including physical education.

Examiner's secrets

You will often be asked to give examples of schemes and programmes used in schools to promote participation among schoolchildren as well as national programmes such as TOPs. You can also use local examples.

Grade booster

Be able to name and describe specific examples of programmes and strategies that are being run in your area as part of the School Sport Partnership programmes.

Checkpoint 4

What advantages might outdoor education have over normal lessons in the inculcation of social skills?

Exam practice answers: page 64

Explain the main differences between an activity that is a sport and one that is physical education. (6 minutes)

Sport and culture

Sport is a reflection of society and many issues (such as class, gender and race) have an effect on sport. Sport follows the trends of society and a number of patterns can be identified.

Culture

Culture is the way the society functions and its traditions and beliefs.

Tribal societies

These are isolated groups of people who live in areas of the world that have not witnessed an industrial or urban revolution.

Examples include the Samoan, Aboriginal and Eskimo cultures.

Characteristics	
Natural	Use what can be found around them
Functional	Activities help to practise skills
Ritual	Linked to worship and religion
Ceremonial	Used to reinforce cultural values of tribe
Survival	Practising hunting and defence skills
Community	Used to select leaders or as initiation in adulthood

Analysis of effects of

→ **Colonialism** – many societies were forced to reject their traditional sports and take up colonial games, often Anglicised versions of cricket and rugby.
→ **Post-colonialism** – since regaining their independence, many societies now combine traditions and customs with modern sport, epitomised by the Samoan 'Haka' in rugby.

Emergent cultures

These are the **developing countries**, such as the African nations. In these countries, modern sport has often been introduced by previous colonial powers and in the main has replaced the indigenous activities. With their new-found independence, the people have used sport as a process of nation building.

The success of countries such as Kenya in athletics, the West Indies in cricket and Brazil in football has shown that developing countries can take on the developed world and often beat them.

These countries face the problems of limited resources and little infrastructure, but through selection and channelling in only a limited number of sports they are able to compete on the world stage. The model of sports development in these countries is shown in the table on the following page.

Grade booster

Try to investigate any links between your own sport and tribal societies

Checkpoint 1

What is meant by the term 'colonialisation'?

Checkpoint 2

Explain the term 'nation building' with relation to sport.

An emergent model of sport

Integration	Sport unites the country by bringing together different races, areas and tribes.
Defence	National Service gives a chance for selection. The strict regime is suited to training and development of talent.
Shop window	Sporting success puts the country onto the world stage.
Selection	There is concentration on a limited number of sports, usually the ones suited to the environment or the physique of the people.

Many emergent countries have now introduced élite sports systems aimed at increasing the chance of gaining gold medals. Often the armed forces act as sports nurseries and screen for sports talent (Kenya is a good example of a country in which the army plays an important role in fostering sports talent).

Performers that do reach an élite level have the opportunity to earn a great deal of money and often move to Western countries, where the opportunity to gain higher reward is greater.

Checkpoint 3

How can the armed forces in emergent cultures play a role in nurturing sports science?

Ethnic sports

These are traditional events that are unique to a particular geographical or cultural area. Examples include the Highland Games in Scotland, various forms of mob football played throughout the UK, hurling in Cornwall and wrestling in Cumberland and Devon.

Checkpoint 4

Define the term 'ethnic sport'.

Characteristics	
Festival	Often annual events that are used to celebrate both religious and secular occasions
Local	Confined to a small geographical area, often as small as just one village or town
Traditional	Have been played for many years, involve local customs
Isolated	Areas are often in more rural areas, away from major conurbations

Reasons for the survival of many for these ethnic sports includes attracting tourism to areas and also a desire by local communities to retain elements of their ethnic identity.

Exam practice   answers: page 64

How can sport be used for social mobility by emergent athletes?   (6 minutes)

Sport in advanced societies

Sport plays an important role in advanced societies, reflecting the wider values and traditions of the society. Most advanced cultures follow a capitalist economy, where private ownership dominates and the market drives most aspects of life, including sport. Increasingly, sport in advanced cultures is seen as a commodity, a chance for companies and individuals to make large amounts of money.

The American model

Checkpoint 1

Explain what is meant by the term 'American Dream'.

In the American model, the sports are high scoring and action-packed to maximise their entertainment value. They reflect American culture in that the aim is to win – the win ethic is what drives all American people and this fuels the so-called 'American Dream'. But it is the commercial aspect of American sport which makes it so different. Every level, from professional national teams to the local high-school football teams, is run as a business. The influence of television is total and most sports in the USA rely entirely on the money generated through television deals and advertising revenue. Sports stars in America are millionaires; most professional teams will have a number of players on multi-million-dollar annual contracts. Many stars, like Michael Jordan, make even more money through sponsorship deals and endorsements.

The jargon

Americanisation means the invasion of American trends and attitudes into traditional culture. Many of these trends are beginning to filter into British sport, and it may be very difficult for us to prevent Americanisation of our sport.

There is a flip side to this: sport in the USA is extremely élitist. In athletics, for example, there is not even one amateur club where 'Joe Public' can train. For most Americans, sport is something you watch on the television and not something you actually play. The television also dictates the rules; for example, American football has evolved into a constant stop–go staccato pattern to allow companies to screen advertisements every five minutes.

Checkpoint 2

Give examples of how British sport is being Americanised.

New World democratic cultures

Australia, South Africa and New Zealand are cultures with European origins and, in the main, former British colonies. Most are under 200 years old and, after achieving independence, developed into advanced thriving societies.

What these countries have in common, apart from a shared colonial history, is a culture of 'Bush Ethos'. The environments remain harsh and the people have had to work hard to develop and expand. Being young countries, they lack the traditions and history of the Old World and have consequently needed to find new ways of expressing their emotions. Sport has more than filled this role: it is often seen as a substitute for the higher forms of culture in Europe.

The other drive is again a form of shop window. The ambition of all these new cultures is to beat their old colonial powers – in particular England. Their sportsmen and women seem to have an extra edge to their approach, are driven by the win ethic and do not appear to be restrained by our more traditional values and ethics. To them, *winning* is important: it reflects struggle and hard work – the values that are inherent in their societies.

Checkpoint 3

Why do New World cultures tend to play sports that originated in the UK?

Checkpoint 4

Why has a country such as Australia placed so much emphasis on developing sports talent?

Exam practice   answers: page 64

The dominant sporting ethic in advanced cultures is that winning is everything. Explain why this win ethic is so strong in modern advanced society.   (8 minutes)

Élite sport

Excellence in sport has two meanings: élitism, which means 'all for the best – forget the rest' or optimum performance, where everyone has the chance to succeed.

Most societies emphasise élitism as this produces champions, which can be used as a 'shop window'. There are three major stages in the development of excellence: selection, development and support. There is much diversity in the methods used by different societies.

Checkpoint 1

Explain what is meant by the term 'shop window'.

An élite sports model

In élitism the emphasis is on a few, the best, performers. The tendency is to look for the most developed and to ignore the rest. We have already seen this approach in the emerging cultures discussed in the previous section. The best example of this approach was seen in the German Democratic Republic, a country with a population of only 16 million which managed to be in the top three for sports such as athletics, swimming and boxing. The whole sports system of this communist country was geared up to selecting and developing champion performers, but this was at the expense of the rest of the population.

The development of excellence

Three key stages may be identified in the development of sporting talent:

1 Selection of talent.
2 Development of talent.
3 Providing support for performance.

The actual methods used differ from country to country, but increasingly a number of policies are being followed by most. A lot of these have been adapted from the Eastern European model of sports excellence, pioneered by the Soviet Union and the German Democratic Republic from the 1950s onwards.

Selection

Selection is the start of this process, identifying individuals with the potential to become champions. The pyramid theory of sports development suggests that the wider the base then the greater the number at the top of the pyramid. The aim of the selection process is to make the base of the pyramid as wide as possible.

Talent development

Stage two is again a crucial aspect. The children selected are coached, instructed and nurtured to become champions. In many countries, this process is achieved through the education system, predominantly in sports schools.

Sports schools

Sports schools are found in most European countries and are often controlled by the state. They allow young people to develop their sporting potential while continuing with academic studies. They usually have high-quality facilities and specialised staff, the advantage being that students get more time to practise their skills and the atmosphere of excellence encourages their development.

Checkpoint 2

List four advantages and four disadvantages of basing performers in sports schools.

Providing support for performance

The final part of the process is to provide support in terms of administration and funding. In many countries, the state funds the top athletes – in Australia, France and the old Soviet Union, all top performers are paid grants that allow them to become virtually full-time athletes. In America, talented performers are paid scholarships by schools and colleges or athletes are contracted to a professional team. In the UK, SportsAid tries to fund up-and-coming athletes – as yet there is little government input to sports in the UK.

Modern sports performers also require the support of an ever-increasing range of sports specialists (psychologists, dieticians, physiotherapists), as well as video and computer equipment to help improve technique. In the UK, such a service is now being developed in a number of National Sports Centres forming a national network, with the United Kingdom Sports Institute (UKSI) as the central focus. The aim is to enable our international performers to use top-quality facilities for training. These now come under the Sports Council's World Class Performance programme, funded by the National Lottery. This Sports Fund has three levels:

Checkpoint 3

What is the role of the UKSI network?

→ **World Class Talent** – programmes aimed at developing talented youngsters.
→ **World Class Development** – assisting with the development of teenagers and helping with educational support.
→ **World Class Podium** – supporting our élite athletes through financial support and providing top-class facilities through the UKSI.

The funding of UK sport is prioritised to ensure the most effective use of lottery funds to achieve the overall aim of the UK being in the world's top five sporting nations.

Checkpoint 4

Describe the three stages in the development of sporting talent.

Grade booster

See if you can research some specific examples of performers at each stage of the World Class Performance programme. Can you find anyone in your local area?

Exam practice   answers: page 64

To achieve excellence in sport, a high level of commitment, resources and expertise is necessary. Describe sporting agencies in the UK who are attempting to assist performers in achieving excellence.   (10 minutes)

Ethics and values in high-level sport

All sports have rules, and deviance occurs when participants break these rules. We call this *cheating* and this is an important issue in modern sport.

Cheating is not a new concept – we know that the ancient Olympians took tonics to try to improve their performances. Some people would argue that cheating is an important element in sport and that without it, sport would be dull.

Sport has many written rules but also *unwritten* rules, and these make investigation of deviance more complicated.

The concept of sportsmanship

Sport relies on **sportsmanship** – people conforming to the written and unwritten rules of sport. The idea of **fair play** means that you treat your opponent as an equal, and although you want to beat them, you will do so only by adhering to the rules and a code of conduct that has been developed in the sport through tradition. This includes shaking hands and cheering the other team off at the end of the game.

To cheat not only destroys the game but also detracts from your personal achievement. A win through cheating is a hollow victory as, although you may gain the extrinsic rewards, you will not gain the more fulfilling intrinsic ones.

Gamesmanship

The alternative dynamic in sport is known as **gamesmanship**, where you use whatever means you can to overcome your opponent. The only aim here is the win, and for most people it is not a question of breaking the rules – more bending them to your advantage.

Violence by spectators

So-called hooliganism in sport is sadly not a new concept. Football is the sport usually associated with crowd disorder and there has been much research and debate about the reasons behind football hooliganism.

Checkpoint 1

Define what is meant by the term 'deviance' in sport.

The jargon

Written rules are sometimes referred to as 'the spirit of the game'; *unwritten rules* are values and ethics which we expect all sportsmen and women to follow.

The jargon

Sportsmanship means conforming to the written and unwritten rules of sport.

The jargon

Fair play means treating your opponent as an equal and abiding by the rules of your sport.

Checkpoint 2

Give examples of the types of extrinsic rewards we can receive in sport.

The jargon

Gamesmanship is where you use whatever means you can to overcome your opponent.

Checkpoint 3

Outline the main differences between sportsmanship and gamesmanship.

Some of the main reasons are:

→ Ritual importance of many football matches such as local derbies where other factors such as religion can be a contributing factor
→ Alcohol
→ Frustration at the result or poor decisions by officials
→ Pre match hype in the media
→ Violence by players on the pitch
→ Poor stadia and ineffective methods of crowd control.

The problem has diminished in recent years, and the increased use of CCTV at football grounds and tighter controls on alcohol are generally seen as key factors in this.

Drugs in sport

Drug abuse has been one of the main areas of deviance in sport during the last few years. It is not clear whether the actual level of drug taking has gone up or whether we now know more about it because testing systems have improved. It is also very difficult to decide where the line should be drawn between illegal and legal substances – many athletes have tested positive but claim that all they took was a cough mixture or other such product which can be bought over the counter.

Drug taking is the ultimate in gamesmanship – taking something to improve your performance and increase your chances of winning.

> **Checkpoint 4**
>
> What is classed as a 'drug' in sport?

> **Exam practice** answers: page 65
>
> Sport relies on sportsmanship – people adhering to both the written and unwritten rules of the game they are playing. Explain what is meant by the terms 'written' and 'unwritten rules' in sport. (10 minutes)

Sport and mass participation

Sport is a natural part of life, whether you are one of the élite competing for gold medals or just playing for fun and enjoyment. The opportunity to take part in sporting activity should be a basic human right; however, many people suffer constraints that prevent them from taking part. The aim of mass participation is to break down these constraints, whatever they may be, and to encourage as many people as possible to take up sport.

The Sports Council

The Sports Council has four main aims:

1 To increase participation in sport.
2 To increase the quality and quantity of sports facilities.
3 To raise standards of performance.
4 To provide information for and about sport.

In 1994 it was announced that the Sports Council would be reshaped to create two new bodies: the **UK Sports Council** and the **English Sports Council**, rebranded as **Sport England** in 1999. This brings England in line with the other home countries in that it now has its own Sports Council. The UK Sports Council has a coordinating role, ensuring that all councils work in the same direction, and has responsibility for drugs testing and doping control in all UK sport.

Each council is split further into regional and local sports councils, enabling area-specific planning. Funding for the Council comes from the National Lottery Sports Fund, and Sport England receives £200 million per year. This money is used to run the regional councils, fund campaigns and capital projects and provide information services, although most of it is redistributed to sports governing bodies and institutions as grants to be used for increasing sports participation, building new facilities and setting up recreation programmes.

The 'Sport for All' campaign, originally set up in 1972 and still continuing, highlights the value of sport and that it is something to which all members of the community should have access. The campaign initially hoped to increase the opportunities for sport and recreation through developing more facilities, and by informing and educating the public about what was available. Recently, the campaign has become more diverse by targeting groups of the community that remain under-represented in sport. Separate campaigns such as '50+ and All to Play For' (aimed at older people) and 'What's your Sport?' (aimed at women) have followed.

Sport for All in Europe

The concept of **Sport for All** first emerged in the early 1960s in Germany and the Nordic countries. In 1968, the **Council of Europe** initiated the setting up of several projects aimed at encouraging mass participation. Their stated aim was to:

Provide conditions to enable the widest possible range of the population to practise regularly either sport proper or various physical activities calling for an effort adapted to individual capacities.

Checkpoint 1

What are the benefits of mass participation for *individuals*?

Take note

The Sports Council estimate that one in three people in the UK regularly take part in sport.

Checkpoint 2

What are the benefits of mass participation in sport for a *country*?

Checkpoint 3

From where did the concept of 'Sport for All' first emerge in the 1960s?

Growing interest in sport and in the specific development of Sport for All by all European countries led to the adoption of the European Sport for All charter in 1972. This asserted that 'Every individual has the right to participate in sport' and that 'It is the duty of every member state to support financially and organisationally this ideal'.

The main organisation charged with implementing Sport for All has been the Committee for the Development of Sport (Comité Directeur pour le développement du sport), known as the CDDS.

The performance pyramid

The different levels of sport can best be represented as a pyramid, and such a concept is used by many sports organisations in order to develop a continuum of participation from grass roots to élite. The broader the base of the participation then, in theory, the greater the élite pool a society can select from.

Performance pyramid

There are four levels of performance within the pyramid. The foundation level, also known as grass roots level, is mainly associated with young children being introduced to sport and learning the basic or fundamental motor skills. In the UK, schemes such as TOP Sport and Dragon Sport have been used by the sports councils to promote participation at this level.

At the participation level, older children are beginning to play full-scale sport, often for teams based in school or the community. The School Sport Co-ordinators programme and the Sport Education and Step into Sport initiatives are example of strategies used to encourage participation at this level.

The performance level is associated with participants who are committed to performing in formal organised competition at higher club and regional level. Participants will usually train for their chosen sport and are usually members of a local sport club or organisation.

The excellence level is where élite athletes perform at a national and/or international level. For many of these performers, sport is their main focus or career; they receive funds either as a professional or through grants and awards from sports organsiations such as the Sports Lottery Fund.

The jargon

European Charter of Sport for All was set up in 1972. It aims to give every European individual the right to participate in sport.

Checkpoint 4

Name the four different levels of the performance pyramid.

Examiner's secrets

It may be easier to revise if you can use examples from the sport you play when referring to the different levels of the sports pyramid.

Exam practice   answers: page 65

Participation in sport brings benefits for individuals and the community. Explain what some of these benefits may be.   (8 minutes)

Factors affecting participation

Many people do not have equal access to sport, often as a result of discrimination due to cultural variables. We can identify a number of so-called target groups in society. These are groups who consistently find it difficult to access sport and recreation.

Cultural factors

There are five main cultural factors that can lead to discrimination in sport:

→ gender
→ class
→ race
→ age
→ ability.

Discrimination can be said to affect the following areas in sport:

→ provision
→ opportunity
→ esteem.

Provision

Are the facilities that allow you to participate available to you? Living in an inner-city area would discriminate against you because there is little provision in these areas. Equipment is also required, which is often expensive – those on low incomes may be discriminated against unless equipment is available free or can be hired cheaply.

Opportunity

There may be barriers to an individual's participation in an activity. In the UK, most sport takes place in the voluntarily run clubs, which are often élitist organisations. Clubs work on membership systems and membership is controlled either by the ability to pay the fees or, in cases such as some golf clubs, election to the club membership. This often closes membership to certain members of the community.

Another consideration for the individual is whether they have the time to play. Women in particular are often faced with this problem. The demands of work and family often mean that women have little leisure time, which accounts in some way for the low levels of female participation in sport.

Checkpoint 1

Explain the three factors that lead to discrimination in sport.

Checkpoint 2

Provision in sport relates to a person's access to what?

Checkpoint 3

How can a sports club act as a barrier to participation?

Esteem

This is concerned with the societal view of individuals. In many cultures, societal values dictate that women should not take an active part in sport, or if they do it should be confined to 'feminine' sports such as gymnastics and not 'macho' pursuits such as football or rugby. These judgements are based on the traditional roles men and women have taken in society and may be very difficult to break.

Stereotypes and **sports myths** are also societal variables that lead to discrimination. Often, minority groups within a community are labelled as having certain characteristics or traits, and this can lead to them being steered into certain sports or positions and away from others.

One good example in the UK is the current lack of Asian footballers in soccer. Much research has been done into this area and programmes are now being set up to try to address the imbalance but the main problem is that, in our societal view, Asians are not potential footballers.

Stereotypes and myths can become 'self-fulfilling prophecies' – even the people they discriminate against come to believe they are valid and conform to the stereotypes by displaying their appointed characteristics and choosing the sports that fit them. In doing so, they are reinforcing society's view. It is only recently that a number of women have broken this system by taking up football and rugby.

The jargon

Stereotypes are a group of characteristics that we believe all members of a certain section of society share, usually based on very little actual fact.

The jargon

Sports myths – stereotypes may lead to myths in sport, and this is where people are discriminated against. Common sports myths are that 'Black people can't swim' and that 'Women will damage themselves internally if they do the hurdles'. Again, myths are based on very little truth, but often become an important aspect in selection and opportunity.

Checkpoint 4

Explain what is meant by the term 'self-fulfilling prophecies' in relation to sport.

Exam practice   answers: page 65

Sport for all is not yet a reality in the UK. How can a person's opportunity to participate in sport be affected by socio-cultural factors?   (9 minutes)

The Olympic Games

The Olympic Games have their origins in Ancient Greece, where they were held every four years as part of a religious ceremony to the god Zeus. At the end of the nineteenth century, Baron de Coubertin reintroduced the Games (the first being held in Greece in 1896), and set up the International Olympic Committee (IOC) and the modern Olympic Games, which are held every four years in a different city.

The modern games

There are actually two Olympic Games – winter and summer – though it is the summer Games that are the most prestigious. De Coubertin's idea was that the Games could be used to bring the people of the world together in friendly competition. He hoped that this might help prevent war and develop more international friendship.

The Olympics in the past have been used to promote the good side of sport. All competitors were amateurs, competing purely for enjoyment, and the winner's medal had no real monetary value. Sportsmanship was the central point of the Games, and before competition started, all the athletes took the Olympic Oath.

The IOC organise each Games every four years, choosing the host city and coordinating funding. Most of the IOC's income now comes from selling the festoon (the five-rings symbol) to international companies and from television fees. Each participating nation must have a national Olympic body that takes responsibility for promoting the Olympic ideals in their own country. In the UK, this is the British Olympic Association.

The British Olympic Association

This independent organisation is responsible for all Olympic matters in the UK, primarily entering competitors for the Olympic Games. Other functions include raising funds to enable British performers to compete at the Games and for the transportation, clothing and other expenses involved in sending a British team (up to £4 million). A more general role is to develop interest in the Olympic movement in Britain. It also helps to coordinate any bids to host the Games.

The jargon

The *International Olympic Committee* is the governing body of the Olympic movement.

Checkpoint 1

What were de Coubertin's ideals behind the setting up of the modern Olympics?

The jargon

Olympic Oath: 'We swear that we will take part in these Olympic Games in the true spirit of sportsmanship and that we will abide by the rules that govern them, for the glory of sport and the honour of our country.'

Checkpoint 2

Explain the link between the Olympic Oath and the concept of sportsmanship.

The jargon

The festoon is the Olympic five-rings symbol, sold to the highest bidders among international companies.

Checkpoint 3

How does the IOC generate most of the funds it needs?

Take note

The 2004 Games were watched on TV by over four billion people worldwide.

The fund-raising role of the British Olympic Association is unique to the UK. In most other countries, even the USA, central government helps to finance the Olympic team – but the British Olympic Association raises all the money itself. This has traditionally been achieved through schoolchildren's sponsored events and donations from the general public and business. Increasingly, more money is being raised through commercial sponsorship, specifically in the use of the Olympic logo (you have probably seen the five-ring logo on Mars Bars and cans of Coca-Cola).

Drugs

Although the essence of the Olympics remains an amateur one, where the only reward winners receive is a token in the shape of an Olympic medal, the commercial opportunities now open to Olympians mean that increasingly many are tempted to use illegal means to improve their performance.

The IOC has, since 1967 when they set up the Olympic Medical Commission, taken the lead role in attempting to prevent the use of drugs in sport. Each year, the IOC produces a list of banned drugs which it then tests for at the Games. Most other sports governing bodies also use this list.

In 2007, USA sprinter Marion Jones was jailed for her involvement in taking performance-enhancing drugs. A winner of several gold medals, she had been drugs tested 120 times over the previous nine years but never failed a test. In court, however, she admitted that she had been taking a steroid called the 'clear' throughout this period. The IOC have since stripped her of her title and medals.

Grade booster

Try to update the examples and case studies you use in your answers. Research what happened at the latest Olympic Games.

Exam practice   answers: pages 65–66

1   What are the reasons for the increasing commercialisation of the Olympic Games?   (10 minutes)
2   *The goal of the Olympic movement is to contribute to building a peaceful and better world.* The Olympic Charter. Comment on the effectiveness of this claim.   (10 minutes)

Issues at the Olympics

In the past, the Olympics were used to promote all that was good in sport. All competitors were amateurs, competing purely for enjoyment and although the winners received a medal it had no monetary value. However, as the modern Games moved into the second half of the twentieth century, television, especially, opened up a huge global audience. This had the effect of making the Games very attractive to commercial sponsors but also gave nations, groups and individuals a world stage on which to make their point.

Women at the Olympics

Women were not allowed to compete in the Ancient Games and when de Coubertin revived the modern Games in 1896 he too upheld this feature. Women did, however, compete at the 1900 Games, but only in two sports – tennis and golf. Gradually, the number of women competing and events open to women has increased, though by 1936 there were still only four sports available to women.

By the time the Olympics were held in Sydney in 2000 there were 28 sports and 116 events for women. There were, however, still twice as many male competitors as women.

Much of the early reluctance to allow women to compete at the Games was due to the philosophy of Baron de Coubertin, the founder of the modern Games. De Coubertin's opinions on women and sport were influenced by the model of the Ancient Greek Games.

There were no women at the Ancient Greek Games – either as competitors or spectators, and in the early years of the modern Olympics the prevailing social pattern was still inclined towards keeping women very firmly in their domestic place. Fortunately, in England, Europe and the USA, women had begun to involve themselves in a range of gymnastic and sporting activities.

The opening of the track and field events to women at the Games of 1928 was highly significant. Annoyed at the refusal of the IOC to include women's athletics in the 1924 Games, a French woman, Alice Milliat, threatened to set up a rival women's organisation. This caused the International Association of Athletics Federations (IAAF) to step in very quickly and endorse women's athletics. The IOC responded by including athletics for women in the 1928 Games which put women's sport at the centre of the Olympic and world stage.

In the 1970s, changing attitudes towards women in society suddenly meant it became acceptable for the sporting female also to be attractive. A host of female athletes like Olga Korbut, Nadia Comaneci and Nelli Kim became household names and helped to promote female participation in sport.

Checkpoint 1

Why do you think that women were allowed to compete in tennis and golf at the 1900 Olympic Games?

Checkpoint 2

Why did the inclusion of track and field events for women at the 1928 Olympics have such a impact on female participation at the Games?

Beauty and grace are still almost unavoidably associated with many women's sporting activities. This, of course, is a societal trait rather than an Olympic one, but it does mean that sports that portray feminine qualities tend to dominate the modern Olympic Games.

Although female participation at the Games is on the up, membership of the IOC is still very much dominated by men.

Politics

The Olympic Games generates a huge media and spectator following which unfortunately means that many have used the Games to make political protests. At one extreme, states have not allowed their athletes to compete in order to make a political point against other competing nations. This is known as a boycott and the Games of 1956, 1976, 1980 and 1984 were severely affected by boycotts.

The essential element of the Olympics is that it brings together athletes and nations of the world. On the whole, this is a very positive experience, reflecting de Coubertin's original ideal of building a more peaceful world through sport.

Smaller groups have used the Games to make more spontaneous statements. At the 1968 Games, two black American sprinters made a 'black power' protest on the podium, knowing that the world's media were watching. Problems such as the terrorist attacks at the 1972 Olympics and later at the 1996 Atlanta Games mean that the security and safety systems at the Olympic Games have become very complex and very expensive.

Using the Olympics as a world stage for protest

© Bettmann/Corbis

Checkpoint 3

What is meant by the term 'boycott' in sport?

Checkpoint 4

In 1964, Rome was the first televised Olympics. What effect did the increased TV coverage of the Games have in terms of protest?

Exam practice   answers: page 66

Explain how and why groups have used the Olympic Games to stage political protests. Refer to an example in your answer.   (10 minutes)

Sport, sponsorship and the media

The most important influence on sport in the twenty-first century is the media. Its impact began in the late nineteenth century with the newspapers and extended into radio coverage in the twentieth century. The radio helped to develop major sporting occasions such as the FA Cup and the Derby into essential elements of our culture. In the 1950s, television transformed many sports into entertainment packages. In the 1990s, satellite added another dimension to sport and made it into a truly global commodity.

The media and sports funding

The presence of the media has turned sport into a commodity that can be bought and sold. Television companies pay out huge amounts of money to cover sports, and advertisers and sponsors back sport because of the exposure they will get in the media. Individuals train and prepare for sport in the knowledge that the media will give them a stage on which to present their talents – and also gain wealth.

Many sports have either been adapted to suit the needs of television or have changed their structure to attract television coverage. In order to survive, a sport needs the media spotlight – without it, it will be left behind.

There is a direct link between the funding of sport and the media. Media coverage brings sponsors and advertising to a sport, which are now essential for a sport to remain viable. Companies sponsor sports mainly as a means of cheap advertising, a way of getting into the public's living room. This is referred to as sport's 'golden triangle' and is becoming increasingly important in the success of sports events.

The influence the media, and specifically television, has over sport is epitomised by the Olympics. This great event is controlled by American television companies, who pay well over $400 million for the exclusive rights to screen the Olympic Games. This kind of financial influence gives the companies control over many factors – for example, we are now used to having to stay up very late to see key moments such as the 100m final so that it fits in with the peak viewing time in America.

Other new innovations include 'pay per view', which involves viewers paying a one-off fee to their cable or satellite supplier in order to watch a particular sports event. This has already been successfully trialled with both boxing and football and looks set to become a regular feature. Another development is the launch of channels specialising in particular sports or sports clubs – Man U TV is already available to fans and offers them 24-hour programming about their favourite football club.

The impact of the media on sport participation

Actual participation in sport appears to be falling, and it has been suggested that the amount of sport now available on the television may have influenced this – people don't play sport because they're too busy watching it. However, other research suggests that television may actually have a positive effect, in that watching sport on the television often stimulates people to take up sports. This effect is very noticeable when British teams are successful in world events such as the Olympics. During the last few years, ice skating, hockey and gymnastics have all witnessed upsurges in popularity when Britons were seen on the television winning medals.

The media, and the press in particular, have turned sportsmen and women into celebrities, which may be beneficial in terms of potential earnings but which also means that they become 'public figures' and their every move, both on and off the pitch, is scrutinised.

There is a general emphasis on sensationalism in the British press where stories (or 'exclusives') are an essential part of the ratings war. All forms of the media are guilty of concentrating on the critical elements of sport – the action replay questioning an official's decision, or viewing a bad tackle or a violent incident from every possible angle. The use of edited highlights, in which only the goals or action is shown, can also give a rather one-sided view of sports.

Modern technology means that no corner of a sport can remain 'hidden'. We now have cameras in the cricket stumps, in the pockets of a snooker table, on cars – giving the armchair spectator the 'real' view. In some cases this has been very beneficial – many of the deviant practices discussed in the last chapter are more closely scrutinised and many sports now use video evidence to pick out any foul play the referee missed in the heat of the game.

> **Checkpoint 2**
>
> How has the influence of the media in sport affected the earning potential of sports stars?

> **Checkpoint 3**
>
> How has the development of media technology helped sports officiate their rules?

The future

Sport has become an important cornerstone of the media and each side feels it has the upper hand, although it would appear that the media is slowly beginning to take control in sport. We have already mentioned that the American networks now own the Olympics, and Sky Television has changed football in the UK from a traditional Saturday game into an almost daily event in order to secure maximum viewing potential.

Rugby league is another sport transformed by satellite television. In 1996, Sky television bought exclusive rights to the game for £85 million, and imposed a number of conditions. The game had to forget 100 years of history and change from a winter sport to a summer game to accommodate television schedules. The leagues were restructured to form a Super League and new clubs have been manufactured in non-rugby league areas in an attempt to widen the market. To aid the marketing, all teams also had to invent nicknames that made them into merchandising commodities and in some way broke down the geographical locations of the games – hence we now have the Bulls *v* the Blue Sox rather than Bradford Northern *v* Halifax!

> **Take note**
>
> In 2007, BSkyB and Setanta paid £1.7bn to screen live Premiership games. Each club in the league received £28 million as part of their share.

> **Exam practice** answers: pages 66–67
>
> What effect does the media have in promoting role models? (6 minutes)

Answers
The social contemporary study of sport

Sport, leisure and recreation: key concepts

Checkpoints

1 Four labour-saving devices that have enabled people who do housework to have more leisure time are: washing machines, dishwashers, tumble dryers, microwaves.
2 A definition of leisure, for professional sports performers, is difficult because these people work within the leisure industry and there is no demarcation between leisure and work.
3 Factors that have led to an increased participation in outdoor sports are: increase in car ownership and ease of access. TV programmes and fashion have also made it popular among young people.
4 The advantages of outdoor education over normal lessons in the inculcation of social skills are: decision making is more important in outdoor education, there is always an element of risk.

Exam practice

Sport is a competitive activity, undertaken freely by individuals and groups, it has set rules and time constraints. Physical education takes place within educational institutions and involves a teacher passing on knowledge to a group of pupils.

Sport and culture

Checkpoints

1 Colonialisation was the invasion and control of developing cultures by the British Empire during the nineteenth century.
2 Nation building, with relation to sport, means using sporting success to motivate and develop pride among a country's population. Sporting success can also enhance a country's international reputation.
3 Often the armed forces act as sports nurseries by providing training and equipment for élite performers and they can also screen for sports talent.
4 Ethnic sports are traditional events that are unique to a particular geographical or cultural area.

Exam practice

Sport can be used for social mobility by emergent athletes because sport can bring extrinsic rewards in terms of money and social status. Many emergent athletes will move to the West where contracts are more lucrative and fees are much higher.

Sport in advanced societies

Checkpoints

1 The American Dream is the idea that anyone in America can move from rags to riches. It is a reflection of a meritocracy – the harder you work the more you are rewarded.
2 Examples of British sport being Americanised are: teams now have nicknames and logos, cheerleaders, entertainment, increasing power of TV.
3 New World cultures tend to play sports that originated in the UK because they were all former colonies of the British Empire.
4 Australia has placed emphasis on developing sports talent because their sporting success counteracts their country's lack of tradition and history.

Exam practice

The win ethic dominates as it reflects the Americanisation of sport. A capitalist society tends to reinforce the 'survival of the fittest' mentality. Commercialism is based on success – advertisers only want to be associated with successful athletes. A business attitude now dominates sport – win or bust.

Élite sport

Checkpoints

1 The term 'shop window' means that sport is used to show off a country.
2 *Advantages* – use best possible resources and facilities for training; have access to quality coaching, often on a one-to-one basis; work in an atmosphere of excellence, surrounded by talented performers; sports science support will be available.

   Disadvantages – away from home, family and friends; chance of burn-out or over-use injuries; out of traditional club network; less emphasis on academic education.
3 The UKSI network allows international performers to use top-quality facilities for training.
4 Three key stages in the development of sporting talent are:
   1 Selection of talent.
   2 Development of talent.
   3 Providing support for performance.

Exam practice
Commitment
National Lottery/World Class Performance funds/national governing bodies are giving athletes grants to allow them to train full time. Many schools and colleges are now developing academies so that students can combine study and élite sport preparation.

Resources
The UKSI network of institutes provides athletes with top-class training facilities and monitoring equipment. Lottery funding is also available for equipment.

Expertise
Lottery and World Class funding have appointed a number of full-time coaches and performance directors. There is also a wealth of expertise and talent at each of the UKSIs.

Ethics and values in high-level sport

Checkpoints

1 The term deviance, when used in sport, means that participants break the rules.
2 Extrinsic rewards in sport can include money, trophies, cups and medals, sponsorship deals, league points.
3 Sportsmanship is playing to the rules and spirit of the game whereas gamesmanship is using whatever means you can to overcome your opponent.
4 A drug in sport is any chemical substance that is taken to improve performance.

Exam practice

Written rules are those published and agreed by the sports governing body. Often, there will be an official referee or umpire to uphold these rules. If a player breaks these rules, they will be penalised or punished. Unwritten rules, often referred to as the 'spirit of the game', require players to respect their opponents and officials, play competitively but fairly and recognise that to win by unfair advantage undermines sport. Shaking hands with your opponent at the end of the game is an example of the unwritten rules.

Examiner's secrets

Make sure you can differentiate between sportsmanship and gamesmanship. This is a popular exam focus. It is often easier to give examples of each concept and then give a definition.

Sport and mass participation

Checkpoints

1 The benefits of mass participation in sport for *individuals* include improvements to fitness and health, self-confidence and a feeling of achievement.
2 The benefits of mass participation in sport for a *country* include a fitter and healthier population, integration of different cultures and races, reduction in crime, economic benefits and a feeling of national pride.
3 The concept of Sport for All first emerged from the Nordic countries and Germany.
4 The four levels of the performance pyramid are: foundation, participation, performance and excellence.

Exam practice

Possible benefits for individuals and the community through participation in sport include:

Individuals – feeling fitter, improvement in health and lifestyle, less likely to suffer from illness or disease, developing sense of achievement/self-esteem/confidence.

Community – fitter population, fitter workforce, less money needed to be spent on healthcare, productivity at work should increase, reduction in crime/antisocial behaviour, feeling of pride in community.

Examiner's secrets

With this type of question it is easy to forget to give answers for both of the parts of the question. Always read the question through carefully a number of times

Factors affecting participation

Checkpoints

1 Three factors that lead to discrimination in sport are:
   1 Provision – where to play
   2 Opportunity – chance to play
   3 Esteem – what the performer will feel like.
2 Provision in sport relates to a person's access to facilities and sport equipment.
3 Sports clubs can act as a barrier to participation because they work on membership systems and membership is controlled either by the ability to pay the fees or, in cases such as some golf clubs, election to the club membership. This often closes membership to certain people in the community.
4 Self-fulfilling prophecies develop from stereotypes and myths, which the people they discriminate against come to believe are valid. They then conform to the stereotypes by displaying their appointed characteristics and choosing the sports that fit them.

Exam practice

A person's opportunity to participate in sport can be affected by socio-cultural factors. For instance, a number of personal factors can affect access to sport. These include gender, age, social status, ethnic background and disability. Provision (where to play), opportunity (chance to play) and esteem (what the performer will feel like) are also relevant.

The Olympic Games

Check points

1 De Coubertin's ideals behind the setting up of the modern Olympics were to promote international friendship through sports competition.
2 The Olympic Oath reinforces the concept of sportsmanship, playing to the laws and spirit of sport, a key feature that de Coubertin wanted to promote at the Games.
3 The IOC generates most of the funds it needs from commercial sponsorship from the TOP sponsors and media fees.

Exam practice

1 The Games now attract a huge global audience and this attracts commercial sponsors. The cost of the Games now runs into billions. Cities or states are unable to fund this without commercial input. In 1984, Uberroth showed that the Games could make a profit through the TOP programme and media fees.

2 The Games are still the largest gathering of people and are watched by 90 per cent of the world's population, but wars have continued throughout the modern Olympic era and many Games have been disrupted by political protest. Many states now see sporting success as a major focus for national building.

Issues at the Olympics

Checkpoints

1 Women were allowed to compete in tennis and golf at the 1900 Olympics because these sports were considered feminine and acceptable by society and the IOC.
2 The inclusion of track and field events for women at the 1928 Olympics had a big impact on female participation at the Games because the number of different events in track and field meant that the number of female participants was bound to increase considerably.
3 The term 'boycott' in sport is the refusal of a country to compete in an international sports event, usually for political reasons.
4 Increased TV coverage of the Games meant that the amount of protest increased as groups recognised the huge live audience their message could now reach.

Exam practice

How – groups have used the Games to make symbolic protest within the Olympic stadium and national teams have undertaken systematic protests involving boycotting the Games.

Year	Host city	Description of protest
1936	Berlin	Germany's leader, Hitler, used the Games to showcase his Nazi views and the power of the German nation.
1968	Mexico City	Two American sprinters used the medal podium to make their 'black power' protest to show their support of the civil rights campaign in the USA. Millions worldwide saw the protest live on TV.
1972	Munich	Palestinian terrorist took several Israeli athletes hostage in the Olympic village to protest about Israel's occupation of Arab territory. In the eventual shootout with police, nine athletes were killed. Many felt the Games should be abandoned in honour of the dead athletes, but the IOC decided the Games should carry on, in order not to be seen to give in to terrorism.

Year	Host city	Description of protest
1976	Montreal	The Games were boycotted by several African countries in protest against New Zealand's presence at the Games after they had played a number of rugby matches against South Africa, who at the time were banned from international sport due to their racist policy of apartheid.
1980	Moscow	The USA led a large boycott of the Games in protest at the Soviet Union's invasion of Afghanistan.
1984	Los Angeles	In retaliation for the USA-led boycott of the Moscow Olympics, the Soviet Union led an Eastern bloc 'tit for tat' boycott of the Games.
1988	Seoul	Three countries boycotted the Games in protest at North Korea not being allowed to host any part of the Games awarded to South Korea.
1996	Atlanta	A terrorist bomb killed several people enjoying a concert outside the Olympic stadium.
2000	Sydney	Cathy Freeman became the first indigenous person in Australia to light the Olympic flame.

Why – the Games are a global event that attract a worldwide audience, and most TV companies carry live coverage, giving protests more impact. A state pulling out of sport does not affect trade or cost them any money.

Examiner's secrets

Where you are instructed you must refer to specific examples in your answer, though it is good practice to do this anyway.

Sport, sponsorship and the media

Checkpoints

1 Television companies pay out huge amounts of money to cover sports, and advertisers and sponsors back sport because of the exposure they will get in the media.
2 The influence of the media in sport has greatly increased the earning potential of sports stars in sports that have high exposure on the television.
3 Modern technology means that no corner of a sport can remain 'hidden'. We now have cameras in the cricket stumps, in the pockets of a snooker table, on cars, giving the officials the 'real' view. Many sports now use video evidence to pick out any foul play the referee missed in the heat of the game.

Exam practice

The media puts sports stars in the public eye and so
creates role models. Success in sport can motivate
others to follow and take up those sports. Commercial
companies also recognise this role-model status and
use sports stars to endorse and advertise their products.
So-called 'household' names can sell almost any product
and so their earning potential is greatly enhanced.

Revision checklist
The social contemporary study of sport

By the end of this chapter you should be able to:		
1 Discuss the key concepts used in the sociological study of sport.	Confident	Not confident **Revise** page 44
2 Give example of schemes and programmes used in schools to promote participation among schoolchildren.	Confident	Not confident **Revise** page 45
3 Explain how sport reflects the culture and society in which it is played.	Confident	Not confident **Revise** page 46
4 Define the ethics and values evident in high-level sport.	Confident	Not confident **Revise** pages 52–53
5 Define what is meant by the term 'deviance' in sport.	Confident	Not confident **Revise** page 52
6 Define and trace the development of the term 'sportsmanship'.	Confident	Not confident **Revise** page 52
7 Discuss how the increasing commercialism of sport is affecting the ethics of sport.	Confident	Not confident **Revise** page 52
8 Discuss the issue of drugs in sport.	Confident	Not confident **Revise** page 53
9 Describe the structure and role of the Sports Councils in the UK.	Confident	Not confident **Revise** page 54
10 Discuss the concept of 'Sports for All'.	Confident	Not confident **Revise** page 54
11 Explain the benefits of mass participation for a country.	Confident	Not confident **Revise** pages 54–55
12 Describe the different sections of the performance pyramid.	Confident	Not confident **Revise** page 55
13 Explain how talented performers are nurtured and supported in the UK.	Confident	Not confident **Revise** page 56
14 Discuss the factors that affect a person's access to sport and recreation.	Confident	Not confident **Revise** pages 56–57
15 Explain the application of the terms: opportunity, provision and esteem.	Confident	Not confident **Revise** pages 56–57
16 Describe how stereotypes and sports myths can lead to discrimination.	Confident	Not confident **Revise** page 57
17 Give an overview of the development of the Olympic Games.	Confident	Not confident **Revise** pages 58–59
18 Describe the structure and philosophy of the modern Olympics.	Confident	Not confident **Revise** pages 58–59
19 Explain the history of women's involvement in the Olympics and how this reflects women's role in society.	Confident	Not confident **Revise** pages 60–61
20 Discuss how states and groups have used the Games to make political protests.	Confident	Not confident **Revise** page 61

Exercise physiology

The energy for physical activity is released by the breaking down of adenosine triphosphate (ATP). This energy source is only stored in small amounts within the body. Consequently, the body must continually reproduce ATP so that we can continue to exercise. We need to review the three methods of ATP production in the body and be able to apply the energy continuum to sporting examples.

Exam themes

- Understanding the types of energy used in the body
- The energy continuum
- ATP – its role and resynthesis
- Compare the aerobic and anaerobic energy systems
- Investigate the energy continuum
- Fatigue and recovery from exercise
- The process of fitness testing
- The principles of training
- The components of fitness and training
- Developing the body's aerobic capacity
- Strength training
- The use of ergogenic aids in improving performance

Topic checklist

	Edexcel		AQA		OCR		WJEC	
	AS	A2	AS	A2	AS	A2	AS	A2
Energy concepts		●		●		●	○	
Fatigue, recovery and training		●		●		●	○	
Aerobic capacity and strength training	○	●	○	●		●	○	
Flexibility	○		○	●				●

Energy concepts

The body needs a constant supply of energy in order to perform everyday tasks, but when we exercise, the rate at which our body uses energy increases. The efficiency of the energy supply is one of the major factors determining athletic performance.

The energy systems

Checkpoint 1

What form of energy is ATP and what form of energy can it be converted into?

There are three ways of synthesising ATP (adenosine triphosphate) from ADP (adenosine diphosphate) and free phosphate to ensure a constant supply of energy. All three systems work together, the dominance of any one depending on the rate at which energy is used. When the demand for energy is high and immediate then the anaerobic processes are heavily relied on. When the demand for energy is low but sustained then the aerobic process is mainly used.

The body takes in chemical energy in the form of the food we eat. This then is converted into kinetic energy which gives us movement, or is stored as potential energy.

ATP – its role and resynthesis

Adenosine triphosphate (ATP) is the only usable form of energy in the body. It is a high-energy phosphate compound made up of one molecule of adenosine and three phosphates.

ATP = adenosine–phosphate–phosphate–phosphate

The bonds that hold the compound together are a source of quite a lot of potential energy. When ATP is broken down, the bonds between the molecules are broken and energy is released. The enzyme ATPase helps to break down ATP. It is broken down into adenosine diphosphate (ADP) and free phosphate (P), so releasing the stored energy.

In order to resynthesise ATP, we need to reverse the process. This is called an **endothermic** reaction since it needs energy to work.

ADP + P + **Energy** → ATP

Take note

The breakdown of ATP:
ATP → ADP + P + **Energy**

There are three ways in which ATP can be resynthesised in the body:

1 The phosphocreatine system (ATP/PC) or alactic system.
2 The lactic acid system or glycolysis.
3 The aerobic process.

Grade booster

Be able to apply the three energy pathways to specific skills or actions in your own sport.

Systems 1 and 2 are anaerobic processes: they take place without oxygen. System 3 is aerobic: it requires oxygen to work.

The phospho-creatine system (ATP/PC) or alactic system	The enzyme *creatine kinase* breaks down the phosphocreatine to phosphate and creatine energy is released	Phosphocreatine $\rightarrow$ P + creatine + **energy**
The lactic acid system or glycolysis	This process involves the *partial* breakdown of glucose, glucose-6-phosphate is formed, the enzyme phosphofructokinase aids the process	Glucose $\rightarrow$ pyruvic acid $\rightarrow$ lactic acid + 2 ATP
The aerobic system	Stage 1 aerobic glycolysis (same as anaerobic glycolysis)	Glucose $\rightarrow$ pyruvic acid $\rightarrow$ lactic acid + 2 ATP
	Stage 2 Krebs cycle	Pyruvic acid + CoA $\rightarrow$ Acetyl CoA + oxaloacetic acid = 2 ATP + hydrogen removed
	Stage 3 electron transport chain	High-energy carbon bonds break to form carbon dioxide and water as well as producing energy to resynthesise 34 molecules of ATP The total yield of the aerobic system is 38 molecules of ATP

Examiner's secrets

You will not be expected to know the detailed pathways of each energy system but you need to have a basic overview and specifically the link between each energy system and the duration and intensity of exercise.

Checkpoint 2

Name and describe the three processes that are used to synthesise ATP.

Checkpoint 3

Where specifically in the body does aerobic glycolysis take place?

The jargon

Glycolysis means the breakdown of glucose.

The energy continuum

We never just produce energy from one source, but tend to use a mix of systems, the degree of utilisation depending on the duration and intensity of the exercise we are undertaking. The different demands are placed on a continuum, with activities requiring 100 per cent aerobic metabolism at one end and those requiring 100 per cent anaerobic metabolism at the other end. The point where we switch from one system to another is called a threshold. Traditionally, the anaerobic threshold has been linked to the onset of blood lactate (OBLA). This is the point where blood lactate begins to accumulate significantly above resting levels.

Examiner's secrets

Very often questions will use a 1500m track race as an example, as this would require a mix of systems.

Checkpoint 4

What is meant by the term 'lactate threshold'?

Exam practice   answers: page 78

1   Describe how the energy pathways of the body work together to produce the energy required by a top-class 1500m runner.   (10 minutes)

2   Name and describe the phase after an intense burst of exercise lasting around a minute.   (7 minutes)

Grade booster

You need to be able to apply ATP resynthesis and energy continuum to practical sports situations.

Fatigue, recovery and training

Fatigue is the exhaustion of muscle resulting from prolonged exertion; recovery is the process of returning the body to its pre-exercise state. During exercise, energy stores are used and waste products created, some of which, such as lactic acid, must be removed.

The process of recovery

Replenishment of ATP and phosphocreatine stores and removal of lactic acid will take place only when additional energy is available. Elevated rates of respiration during recovery provide the energy for these processes and this in turn results in a state of EPOC.

Myoglobin acts as a store of oxygen during strenuous exercise but during intense exercise the myoglobin stores of oxygen are depleted – it takes about 0.5 litres of oxygen and one to two minutes to replenish these stores. Energy is not required for this process, but it will happen only when a 'surplus' of oxygen is being delivered to the muscles. During recovery, the elevated rate of ventilation and heart rate means that additional oxygen is available for myoglobin replenishment.

The jargon

Excess post-exercise oxygen consumption (EPOC) is the extra oxygen needed to restore the body to its pre-exercise state.

Checkpoint 1

What is the purpose of recovery?

Fitness testing

A variety of tests are used to assess a performer's fitness levels. We will identify these as we revise each of the main fitness components below. Performers can undergo fitness testing before, during and after a training programme. Testing at these times can achieve four important benefits: identifying specific strengths of a performer, identifying any weaknesses, monitoring progress and providing motivation and incentive. Prior to undertaking any fitness testing, performers must follow safety procedures and precautions to ensure that they are physiologically and psychologically prepared. In order to assess this readiness, performers will be asked to complete a Physical Activity Readiness Questionnaire (PARQ).

Checkpoint 2

What is the role of a PARQ?

Principles of training

A training programme should be devised to fit individual needs. This is called systematic, one sportsperson may have more time than another person. One person may be more motivated than another person. One person's position in a team may be different from another person's. Principles of training are simply training rules that apply to the training of all the sports they attempt, to ensure that training is safe and produces the desired physiological adaptations.

Use the word SPORT to remember the five principles of training.

| S | SPECIFICITY | Your training is geared 'specifically' towards your sport and/or your particular position and time in season |
| P | PROGRESSION | Gradually increase your training programme in order take yourself onto a higher level of fitness |

O	OVERLOAD	Train at a worthwhile range of intensity (also known as training in your *target zone*)
R	REVERSIBILITY	If you train less or if you stop training because of injury, you will lose fitness
T	TEDIUM	Make the sessions different and enjoyable. When boredom sets in it is very difficult to motivate yourself to improve your fitness

Linked to the above is the FITT principle.

F	FREQUENCY	How many times per week you need to train in order to improve your fitness
I	INTENSITY	How hard you train. Train at an intensity that will take your pulse into the *target range*
T	TIME	How long each session must be in order to be of any benefit and to achieve improvement
T	TYPE	What sort of training you do

The components of fitness and training

There are five principle training methods:

→ **Interval training** – Involves periods of work followed by periods of rest.
→ **Continuous training** – In continuous training, you do not stop working.
→ **Fartlek training** – Means '*speed play*', a combination of fast and slow running.
→ **Circuit training** – Involves a number of exercises set out so you avoid exercising the same muscle group consecutively.
→ **Weight training** – Uses progressive resistance, either in the form of actual weight lifted or in terms of the number of times the weight is lifted.

Included in any training schedule are:

1 The number of exercises.
2 The exercises for each muscle group.
3 The weight/intensity of the effort used.
4 The number of repetitions.
5 The number of sets.
6 How fast the exercise is done.
7 How long the rest is between sets.
8 The frequency of training.

Checkpoint 3

What is meant by the term 'target zone'?

Checkpoint 4

What is the difference between maximal and sub-maximal training and testing?

Grade booster

Be able to apply the components of fitness and training in both a power athlete and an aerobic athlete.

Exam practice   answers: page 78

1 What precautions and procedures should an athlete follow before undertaking any form of fitness testing?   (5 minutes)

2 Outline the methods an athlete can employ to aid their recovery after intense physical activity.   (7 minutes)

Aerobic capacity and strength training

Cardiovascular fitness is the ability to exercise the entire body for long periods of time. It requires a strong heart and clear blood vessels to supply the muscles with plenty of oxygen via the blood. Cardiovascular fitness has some benefit to all sports people as it concerns the fitness of the most important muscle in the body, the heart.

The best measure of cardiovascular fitness is called maximum oxygen uptake or VO_2 max. This measures the ability of the heart, lungs and blood to transport oxygen to the muscles. It can be measured using a number of fitness tests but the most common is the multi-stage fitness test which gives athletes a predicted VO_2 max.

Checkpoint 1

How is maximum oxygen uptake usually presented in a shortened form?

The multi-stage fitness test

This test involves running back and forward along a 20-metre zone. The speed of running is controlled by a series of pre-recorded beeps played back through a CD or cassette player. The aim of the test is to run for as long as possible, continuing until you are unable to keep up with the beeps. The level at which you stop running gives you your cardiovascular score, which can then be converted to give a predicted VO_2 max. Criticism of the test points to the fact that motivation plays an important part in how long the performer keeps running. It is also very specific to running sports. Other common tests used to measure aerobic capacity are the Harvard step test and the 12-minute Cooper Run.

Grade booster

Be able to give figures for VO_2 max. The average for a male is between 40 and 45 ml/kg/min. David Beckham has a VO_2 max of 83 ml/kg/min.

Physiological adaptations of aerobic training

The aim of all training methods is to produce long-term physiological adaptations.

Sustained aerobic training should result in the following physiological adaptations:

The jargon

Hypertrophy is an increase in the size of a tissue or organs.

→ Hypertrophy of the myocardium.
→ Increase in stroke volume and cardiac output.
→ Decrease in resting heart rate.
→ Increase in lung volume and maximum minute ventilation.
→ Increase in blood volume and elasticity of the vascular system.
→ Increase in muscle myoglobin and the number of mitochondria and stores of energy.

Checkpoint 2

Describe how an increase in stroke volume and cardiac output would have a beneficial effect on aerobic capacity.

Strength

Strength is the ability of a muscle to exert force and overcome resistance. It is an essential element of many sporting skills. There are a number of different types of strength.

Type of strength	Description	Sports application
Strength endurance	The ability of a muscle to work for a long period of time	Press-ups
Maximum strength	The greatest force that can be exerted in a single maximum voluntary contraction	Bench press in weight training
Explosive strength	The ability to expend energy on one explosive act	Javelin throw
Static/isometric strength	The greatest amount of force held for a period of time	Rugby scrum
Dynamic strength	The ability to exert muscular force repeatedly over time	Sprinting

Strength can be measured by a number of methods: the most common are maximal lift or using a grip dynamometer. Endurance strength can be measured using the sit-up test developed by Sports Coach UK. Dynamic strength can be measured using the vertical jump test.

Physiological adaptations of strength training

Depending on the intensity and duration of the sessions, strength training can produce both aerobic and anaerobic adaptations. Aerobic adaptation would result from low weights and many repetitions, which could result in hypertrophy of the slow-twitch muscle fibres, an increase in muscle mitochondria and myoglobin, capillarisation and a general increase in energy stores.

Checkpoint 3

Give three examples in sport that require static, explosive and dynamic strength.

Checkpoint 4

What is capillarisation and what beneficial effect does it have in terms of the cardiovascular system?

The jargon

Capillarisation is the development of the capillary network in a part of the body.

Action point

Make sure you can identify the energy system that would be utilised by each type of strength.

Exam practice   answers: page 78

Outline the long-term physiological adaptations in the skeleton, muscular and circulatory systems that would occur as a result of marathon training.

(10 minutes)

Flexibility

This type of fitness links both the muscular and skeletal systems. Muscles that are not stretched regularly become tight, causing pain when we stretch them. Flexibility is important in most sports, as not only does it allow a greater range of movement but it also helps prevent injury.

Types of flexibility

There are a number of types of flexibility:

→ **Static flexibility** is the range of movement possible around a joint.
→ **Dynamic flexibility** is the range of motion that can be achieved by actively moving a joint by force.

Flexibility can be affected by a range of factors including the joint type and the elasticity and length of the surrounding connective tissue. The most common methods of measuring flexibility are the sit-and-reach test or using a goniometer. A loss of flexibility can be caused by problems in the joints such a worn-down cartilage or a lack of synovial fluid.

There are three main methods of flexibility training:

→ **Static stretching** includes a further two methods: **active** where a joint is stretched by the athlete actively contracting the antagonistic muscles to push the joint past its point of resistance and **passive stretching** which involves using an external force, usually gravity or a partner, to produce the stretch in the muscles.
→ **Ballistic stretching** produces a stretch using bouncing or swinging movements. This should be done with care since it can result in muscle tears and tissue damage.
→ **Proprioceptive neuromuscular facilitation (PNF)** is usually performed with a partner and involves a pattern of alternating contraction and relaxation of the muscles being stretched.

Checkpoint 1

What are the benefits of improving an athlete's flexibility?

Checkpoint 2

Explain why PNF stretching is said to be more effective than other forms of stretching.

Physiological adaptations of flexibility training

The aim of sustained fitness training is to develop elasticity in the tendons, ligaments and muscles surrounding the joints. The resting length of these structures will also be increased.

Other elements of fitness

There are a number of other fitness components that can contribute towards an athlete's fitness. The main ones are shown in the table.

Fitness component	Description	Training methods
Balance	The ability to distribute the weight of the body evenly and maintain equilibrium	Use of balance board or beam
Coordination	The ability to put relevant motor programmes in the right order to produce efficient smooth movement	Ball catch task Batak board
Agility	The ability to rapidly and accurately change the direction of the entire body	Illinois agility run
Reaction time	The ability to respond quickly to a stimulus	Ruler drop Batak board Computer simulators
Speed	The ability to perform a movement quickly	60m sprint Plyometrics

Ergogenic aids

An ergogenic aid is any aid that improves performance. With the demands of modern-day sport and the fact that the difference between winning and losing could be fractions of a second, most élite athletes are constantly looking for aids that can give their performance an edge. There is much debate in sport about the legal and ethical background to the use of ergogenic aids. Currently, the use of a vast number of performance-enhancing drugs is banned. However, a range of supplements and other chemical aids are allowed.

Current examples of ergogenic aids include:

→ Nutrition manipulation
  → carbo-loading
  → taking creatine supplements

→ Boosting the body's red-blood-cell count
  → altitude training
  → blood doping
  → using hypoxic chambers
  → taking banned Rh EPO.

Checkpoint 3

Suggest why agility is such an important component of so many sports.

Grade booster

These elements do need to be studied in depth but it would be useful if you were aware of the contribution they can make to an athlete's performance and also be able to give examples of how they can be improved.

Checkpoint 4

Outline the possible physiological benefits of altitude training in an endurance athlete.

The jargon

Erythropoietin (*EPO*) is a naturally occurring hormone that stimulates red-blood-cell production. A number of athletes have been caught recently taking REPO, a synthetic version, in an attempt to illegally boost their oxygen-carrying capacity.

Action point

Try to keep up to date with the technical developments in sport. You will always get credit for using contemporary examples in your exam answers.

Grade booster

Be able to talk about the use of ergogenic aids in your own sport.

Exam practice   answers: pages 78–79

1 Describe how an endurance athlete might manipulate their dietary plans during the final week before an event.   (10 minutes)

2 Explain the benefits of an athlete taking creatine as a dietary supplement when preparing for competition.   (5 minutes)

Answers
Exercise physiology

Energy concepts

Checkpoints

1 ATP energy is potential/chemical energy and it can be converted into kinetic/mechanical energy.
2 The three processes that are used to synthesise ATP are: the phosphocreatine system (ATP/PC) or alactic system; the lactic acid system or glycolysis; and the aerobic system.
3 Aerobic glycolysis takes place in the mitochondria.
4 The term 'lactate threshold' is the point at which lactic acid begins to accumulate rapidly in the blood, also called the anaerobic threshold.

Exam practice

1 Energy continuum, where activity requires a combination of the energy systems, 1500 metres at an élite level. Four minutes of exercise will use ATP/PC at the start and end of the race. The last stage will also see the athlete use the lactic acid system in the sprint to the line. If most of the race is run at a moderate pace then the aerobic system will supply the majority of the energy required.
2 The lactic acid system, anaerobic glycolysis, glucose is broken down into pyruvic acid, releasing two molecules of ATP for each molecule of glucose used. It supplies energy for high intensity for around one minute.

Fatigue, recovery and training

Checkpoints

1 Recovery is the period following physical activity in which the body's systems repair damaged tissue and replenish energy stores.
2 The role of PARQ (a pre-test questionnaire) is to ensure that performers are physiologically and psychologically prepared for testing.
3 A target zone is a specific level of intensity that an athlete needs to work at to obtain a specific physiological adaptation.
4 Maximal training is where subjects work to exhaustion, whereas sub-maximal training is where an individual works towards a pre-set level which is below their maximum.

Exam practice

1 Athletes should undertake a PARQ and thoroughly warm up before any physical activity. The athlete needs to be physiologically and psychologically prepared for testing or training.
2 Methods to aid recovery include massage which helps stimulate blood flow; a thorough cool-down to prevent blood pooling and help remove the waste products; use of ice baths or ice jackets, again to stimulate blood flow; hot and cold showers to facilitate nervous and vascular activity in the muscles.

Aerobic capacity and strength training

Checkpoints

1 The maximum oxygen uptake is usually presented in the shortened form: VO_2 max.
2 Increased stroke volume means that the volume of blood pumped out of the left ventricle increases and an increase in cardiac output means that there is more blood available to the body, and it is moving faster around the body.
3 *Static strength* – rugby scrum, rings, gymnastics.
   Explosive strength – bounding, jumping for a header in football, lay-up in basketball.
   Dynamic strength – 100m sprinting.
4 Capillarisation is the development of the capillary network in a part of the body, and would include increasing the absolute number of capillaries and the capillary density, which gives a greater surface area available for the transfer of nutrients and waste products so making the vascular system more efficient.

Exam practice

The long-term physiological changes that result from marathon training would include: increased size and number of mitochondria, increased myoglobin, increased fuel stores and oxidative enzymes, increased efficiency of the lungs, hypertrophy of the heart, capillarisation and an increase in blood volume.

Flexibility

Checkpoints

1 The benefits of increased flexibility are that it allows athletes a greater range of movement and they become less susceptible to injury.
2 PNF stretching is more effective since the assisting partner can help put the joint in a full-stretch position and also hold it in that position for 10 to 15 seconds, ensuring that the joint moves through its full range of motion.
3 Agility is important in many sports because it allows the athlete to change direction with maximum speed and control, allowing them to evade defenders or reach a ball.
4 The benefits of altitude training include: increasing haemoglobin content and therefore increased oxygen carrying capacity; decrease in blood plasma volume; capillarisation in the muscles; and an increase in muscle myoglobin.

Exam practice

1 An athlete might manipulate their diet during the final week before an event by carbohydrate loading. This involves depleting and temporarily starving the body of its normal supply of carbohydrates. Glycogen levels will then be low. The body is then saturated with

carbohydrates three days pre-event. When the body is again exposed to normal levels of carbohydrate it will store extra glycogen, helping to extend the duration of activity for endurance events.

2 Creatine increases PC stores in the body and therefore raises the threshold of the alactic system. It specifically aids sport where work is intermittent. The additional creatine improves recovery time. It also allows athletes to train at higher intensity for longer periods of time.

Revision checklist
Exercise physiology

1	Discuss the three ways of synthesising ATP within the body and its application to sport.	Confident	Not confident. **Revise** pages 70–71
2	Explain the term energy continuum and be able to give practical examples of its application in sport.	Confident	Not confident. **Revise** pages 70–71
3	Describe how the knowledge of threshold can aid sports training and performance.	Confident	Not confident. **Revise** pages 70–71
4	Discuss the process of recovery from exercise.	Confident	Not confident. **Revise** pages 72–73
5	Discuss the concept of aerobic capacity and be able to give training methods linked to the concept.	Confident	Not confident. **Revise** pages 74–75
6	Discuss the components of fitness and training.	Confident	Not confident. **Revise** pages 72–77
7	Explain the principles of training.	Confident	Not confident. **Revise** pages 72–73
8	Outline the physiological adaptations of aerobic training.	Confident	Not confident. **Revise** page 74
9	Outline the physiological adaptations of strength training.	Confident	Not confident. **Revise** page 75
10	Explain the importance of flexibility in most sports.	Confident	Not confident. **Revise** pages 76–77
11	Discuss and give training methods for the various fitness components.	Confident	Not confident. **Revise** pages 76–77
12	Give examples of ergogenic aids in sport.	Confident	Not confident. **Revise** page 77

Sports psychology

A successful athlete requires not just a high level of skill and the appropriate physiological conditioning, but also the right mental attitude. Those athletes who are highly skilled and at the top of their fitness for their sport may not perform at their optimal levels if they do not feel confident, are unmotivated or are stressed by the competition. The role of sport psychology is to help performers control their stress levels and emotions, mentally preparing for performance and focussing in on the most important cues for their sport. The main areas of potential limits on performance are motivation, arousal and stress management.

Exam themes

- Personality and attitudes
- Sports psychology and its effect on group performance
- Group dynamics
- Mental preparation for sport
- Leadership in sport
- Effects and consequences of competition
- Emotional control
- Social facilitation and the presence of others
- Aggression
- Attribution theory

Topic checklist

	Edexcel		AQA		OCR		WJEC	
	AS	A2	AS	A2	AS	A2	AS	A2
Sports psychology and its effects on the individual performer			●		●	●		●
Sports psychology and its effects on group performance			●	●	●	●	●	●
Mental preparation for sport		●		●	●	●		●
Effects and consequences of competition		●		●	●	●		●

Sports psychology and its effects on the

Every sports performer is an individual. This makes it very difficult to predict how each person will react in certain situations. However, there are a number of underlying traits that are common to us all and certain environmental influences that appear to affect us in similar ways. In this section we will review the work done on linking individual differences to sports performance.

Personality

There are many different personality types and theories.

Eysenck was one of the first psychologists to investigate personality. He identified two basic types, introverts and extroverts, that can be applied to sports performers.

Extroverts	Introverts
Prefer team sports	Prefer individual sports
Aggressive	Less active
Very competitive	Less competitive

Checkpoint 1

Explain the difference between the trait and social learning approaches to the study of personality.

Trait theories of personality suggest that someone's personality is an enduring trait that influences behaviour in all situations. The narrow band approach splits personalities into two types: Type A personalities are impatient, intolerant and experience high levels of stress, whereas Type B personalities are relaxed, tolerant and have lower stress levels. Another approach, called social learning, suggests that a person's personality changes with the situation and that the environment around the performer influences behaviour. Interactionists believe that both the trait and social learning theories are valid – we are born with certain personality traits but these can change in given situations.

Examiner's secrets

You need to be able to discuss the limitations of personality profiling in sport.

Attitudes

Attitudes are learnt predispositions that make us act in a particular way in a given situation. The triadic model identifies three types of influence that form attitudes:

Checkpoint 2

Describe the triadic model.

→ Beliefs – the cognitive element
→ Emotions – the affective element
→ Behaviour – the behavioural element.

Attitudes in sport and physical education can be changed through persuasion and through Festinger's theory of cognitive dissonance. This theory suggests that people like to be consistent in their thoughts and attitudes. If two cognitive elements conflict and people are motivated to reduce dissonance, they will feel more comfortable with the positive element and this will become the dominant attitude.

Checkpoint 3

Explain how cognitive dissonance can change attitude.

Attitudes are mainly based around past experience and social learning, especially through vicarious experience, and we tend to follow social norms.

Often stereotypes and sporting myths can shape our behaviour.

The jargon

Vicarious experience is experience gained by watching other people perform.

individual performer

Motivation

Motivation is often referred to in two ways:

Intrinsic motivation is the drive to do well which comes from inside yourself, often associated with enjoyment and pride.

Extrinsic motivation is a drive to do well that comes from outside, from, for instance, other people or a form of reward such as money, a prize or a trophy.

Atkinson and McClelland developed the theory of achievement motivation; they identified two types of performer. Some have a greater need to achieve (*Nach*) than others and have what is known as 'approach behaviours'. People at the other end of the scale seem to avoid competitive situations because they need to avoid failure (*Naf*) and have what is known as 'avoidance' behaviours.

Nach athletes tend to	*Naf* athletes tend to
have a persistent attitude – stick to the job in hand	give up easily
be willing to take risks	avoid challenging situations
take responsibility for their actions	avoid personal responsibility
welcome feedback about their performance	not want feedback about their performance

Checkpoint 4

Would you expect *Nach* or *Naf* athletes to avoid competitive situations?

Examiner's secrets

Candidates will be expected to be able to give specific sports examples of achievement motivation.

Exam practice   answers: page 90

Attitude in sport affects the behaviour of both participants and spectators. Describe what is meant by the term 'attitude' and identify influences which might shape the attitude of sports performers and spectators.   (8 minutes)

Sports psychology and its effects on group

Most sports involve groups of people performing together or supporting one another. The way that these people interact and communicate has been the focus of much psychological study. Individuals on teams and in competition will bring their own personalities but they will also be influenced by a range of others including their co-performers on the pitch as well as officials, members of the crowd, family friends and the media.

Group dynamics

Grade booster

Try to use these phrases when answering questions on group dynamics.

Key phrases used when discussing groups and teams are:

Phrase	Explanation
Group dynamics	Processes within the group and between groups
Cohesion	Forces which motivate members to stay and work for the group
Mutual awareness	Understanding of the needs and aims of team members
Interaction	Interplay between members of the group
Common goal	Sharing of an aim or predetermined result

Checkpoint 1

What factors affect group cohesion?

Examiner's secrets

Make sure you can offer suggestions about successful teams.

Steiner developed a model which looks at the processes that operate within a team.

Actual productivity = potential productivity – losses due to faulty processes

Steiner also identified that two main reasons for unproductive groups are coordination problems, such as the Ringleman Effect, and motivational problems, such as social loafing. The Ringleman Effect suggests that individual performance decreases as the group size increases.

Leadership

Checkpoint 2

What is meant by social loafing?

The jargon

Social loafing – where an individual loses motivation within a group. It is linked to a loss of identity.

Checkpoint 3

Describe how a group leader may emerge.

Leaders play an important role in influencing groups and individuals as well as setting goals. In terms of sport, leaders include team captains, coaches, managers and teachers. There is some debate as to whether leadership is a natural trait or influenced by social learning. Carron suggested that leaders can emerge in two ways:

→ **Emergent** – from within a group because they are identified as skilful or responsible
→ **Prescribed** – appointed from an external source.

performance

Many different types of leadership styles have been identified:

Style	Description
Task-orientated	Concerned with the task the group has been given.
Person-orientated	Concerned with interpersonal behaviour of the group.
Authoritarian	Task-orientated and leader-centred – little or no intervention from the rest of the group.
Democratic	Considered – encourages intervention from all team members.
Laissez-faire	Takes very few decisions; lets team members do as they wish.

Take note

Most leaders are actually a mix of all styles, but may tend towards one.

Different sports individuals and groups have their own preferred styles, though again this depends on the situation. Chelladurai identified five categories of preferred leadership styles that can be applied to performers of different ability and experience. These are:

→ training and instruction
→ democratic
→ autocratic
→ social support
→ rewarding.

Again, the actual style of leadership may alter with the situation the group is in. Fiedler's contingency model of leadership applied the dual classification of task- and person-orientated styles to a range of situations. His conclusion was that task-orientated leaders are more effective in situations that are at the extremes of favourable or unfavourable, whereas person-orientated leaders are most effective in situations that are moderately favourable.

Checkpoint 4

What factors would make a situation more favourable for a leader?

Grade booster

Be able to discuss how the theories of sports psychology have traditionally been split between the concepts of nature and nurture.

Exam practice   answers: page 90

1 Identify three leadership qualities that are important in a sports coach.
                                                                (5 minutes)

2 Autocratic and democratic styles are often used by people in a leadership position. Explain each style of leadership and suggest situations which each type may favour.
                                                                (8 minutes)

Mental preparation for sport

Checkpoint 1

Give three examples of typical stressors in sport.

Stress has always been an integral part of sport, though many would argue that the amount of stress in sport in recent years has increased greatly due to the amount of sponsorship and other extrinsic rewards now available to successful performers. To begin reducing the effects of stress, sports performers need first of all to identify the source of stress and then use methods of mental preparation to help them prepare for competition.

Commitment

Goal setting can help improve a performer or team's motivation and confidence, reduce anxiety and ultimately enhance performance. There are three different types of goals:

→ **outcome goals**
→ **performance goals**
→ **process-orientated goals.**

Many élite performers and teams will set themselves long-term goals, for example, over a season, but these will be preceded by short-term goals which help control anxiety. To make goal setting more effective, many now use the guide known as the SMARTER principle.

S	Specific	Goals must be clear and understood
M	Measurable	Performers must be able to check or assess how well they are progressing
A	Agreed	Goals shared with coach and team are more likely to be achieved
R	Realistic	Goals must be within the reach of the performer
T	Time-phased	Short-term goals give a step-by-step move towards long-term goals
E	Exciting	Goals must stimulate and offer rewards
R	Recorded	Goals must be written down and any progress recorded, to help with motivation

Checkpoint 2

Can you think of a sports-specific example of self-efficacy?

The jargon

Performance accomplishments – if success has been accomplished in the past then self-confidence will be high.

Self-confidence

Motivation is often affected by the level of self-confidence a performer has. Bandura proposed a theory of self-efficacy which suggested that self-confidence can be specific to a particular situation. There are a range of factors that affect self-efficacy: performance accomplishments, vicarious experiences, verbal persuasion and emotional arousal.

Concentration

The jargon

Cue – a signal for a particular action. It may be verbal, visual or kinaesthetic.

Being able to concentrate on important cues is an essential trait for sports performers. Cue utilisation theory suggests that as athletes' arousal increases, their attention narrows, initially filtering out irrelevant environmental cues, leading to improved performance.

However, if arousal continues to rise then relevant cues are also ignored, leading to a loss in performance. Psychologists identify a range of additional styles which relate to a two-dimensional model of the direction (external to internal) and width (broad to narrow) of attention.

Emotional control

Sports performance is closely linked to an athlete's level of arousal and activation. There are two main theories about the relationship between arousal level and performance. The drive theory developed by Hull suggests that there is a linear relationship, in that performance increases in proportion to arousal, thus:

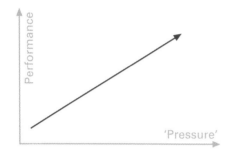

The inverted U theory, developed by Yerkes and Dodson, suggests that optimum performance is reached at moderate arousal levels, but at low and high arousal levels performance decreases. Each individual performer will have a unique level of optimum arousal and this may change according to the situation.

Often athletes become anxious before competitive events. This is referred to as stress and it can have both positive and negative effects on performance. Anxiety is a negative form of stress. There are two types of anxiety: **trait anxiety** – an enduring tendency to exhibit anxiety and **state anxiety** – the anxiety actually experienced in a particular situation. In sport, we are mainly concerned with anxiety associated with competition; Marten developed the SCAT test which can be used to measure competitive anxiety.

Managing stress is therefore an important skill for athletes to master. At the outset, identifying signs of stress are useful. Two types of state anxiety have been recognised: **somatic anxiety** (stress response of the body) and **cognitive anxiety** (stress response of the mind). There are a number of techniques that are useful for controlling both types of anxiety.

Imagery	Visualising success or enjoyment
Self-talk	Using key word and phrases to maintain focus and concentration.
Relaxation	Tensing muscles to relax parts of the body.

Checkpoint 3

How should a coach utilise knowledge of the inverted U theory of arousal when motivating a sports team for an important match?

Checkpoint 4

Describe what is meant by 'state' and 'trait' anxiety.

The jargon

Activation – the state of readiness of an individual to respond to a stimulus or cue.

Grade booster

Many questions will ask for strategies that can be used to reduce anxiety – make sure you have lots of examples.

Exam practice   answers: page 90

1 Anxiety is the negative aspect of stress. Explain what is meant by the terms 'somatic' and 'cognitive' anxiety. (5 minutes)
2 Name and describe one cognitive technique of stress management.

(4 minutes)

Effects and consequences of competition

Competition is the main focus for most people in sport and this brings in another range of factors that affect confidence and motivation. The presence of others raises arousal levels which can have either a positive or negative effect on performance. Again, in order to be successful, performers need to identify the effects that competition can have on their own performance and then develop coping strategies to deal with any negative effects.

Social facilitation and audience effect

Social facilitation is the influence other people can have on an individual's performance. These 'others' could include other performers/co-actors or an audience, either live or via TV. Zajonc suggests that the presence of others raises arousal levels, which can have a positive or negative effect on performance, and this can be linked to drive theory, with the dominant response being more likely in high-arousal situations. This would create a positive response for experts, extroverts or during activities using simple or gross skills, but would produce a negative response in beginners, introverts and during activities using fine and complex skills. The presence of others can also cause evaluation apprehension where others are evaluating performance.

Aggression

Aggression is a term that is loosely used in sport. Again, it can have both a positive and negative effect on performance. Aggression is literally 'intent to harm outside the laws of the game'. Where aggression is controlled or channelled it becomes assertion and it is this concept we should encourage in sport.

There are a number of theories that suggest causes for aggression and they tend to fall into the two camps of **nature** or **nurture**. The instinct theory suggests that aggression is an innate biological drive and sport simply gives an outlet for this aggression. The frustration–aggression hypothesis is a version of the drive theory which states that blocking goals can cause frustration which then leads to aggression. The social learning theory developed by Bandura states that we learn to be aggressive by watching others. Strategies to reduce aggression include internal control of arousal levels, punishment and the reinforcement of non-aggressive behaviour.

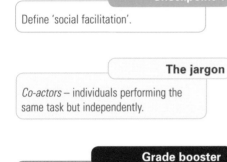

Checkpoint 1

Define 'social facilitation'.

The jargon

Co-actors – individuals performing the same task but independently.

Grade booster

It is important that you are able to give examples of strategies to reduce the influence others have on performance.

Checkpoint 2

Explain the differing theories that suggest how aggression is caused.

Consequences of sports performance

Attribution theory

Attributions are the reasons we give for winning or losing. They can be linked to motivation and therefore have an important effect on future performance. Weiner developed a model which gives four main reasons for a result, thus:

Locus of causality

	Internal cause	External cause
Stable cause	Ability	Task difficulty
Unstable cause	Effort	Luck

Often beginners or performers who do not gain consistent success can develop learned helplessness. Often failure is attributed to uncontrollable factors. Attribution retraining can help to change attributions and minimise the effects of learned helplessness.

Checkpoint 3

What can create learned helplessness in a performer?

Checkpoint 4

In what ways can learned helplessness be changed into a positive attribute?

Exam practice   answers: pages 90–91

For most athletes the presence of an audience leads to a rise in arousal levels. Outline the positive and negative effects that an audience may have on performance and state how this may differ depending on the level of the performer. (10 minutes)

Answers
Sports psychology

Sports psychology and its effects on the individual performer

Checkpoints

1 Trait theories of personality suggest that someone's personality is an enduring trait that influences behaviour in all situations, whereas social learning suggests that a person's personality changes with the situation and that the environment around the performer influences behaviour.

2 The triadic model identifies three types of influence that form attitudes:
→ *Beliefs* – the cognitive element
→ *Emotions* – the affective element
→ *Behaviour* – the behavioural element.

3 Cognitive dissonance can change attitude. By making all three elements stable, and changing attitude, an individual must experience two or more opposing beliefs and make one of these beliefs dominant.

4 *Naf* athletes would tend to avoid competitive situations.

Exam practice

An attitude in sport is a predisposition towards an attitude subject. Influences include previous participant and spectator experiences, vicarious experiences, influence from the media, presence of TV and/or crowd reactions, cultural and religious factors, and the behaviour of peers and significant others.

> **Grade booster**
>
> Always try to write down a couple of extra points. PE examiners are positive markers – you will always get credit for correct answers.

Sports psychology and its effects on group performance

Checkpoints

1 Factors that affect group cohesion include having shared goals, success of performance, level of social friendship and the effectiveness of the leadership.

2 Social loafing is the reduction in individual effort and motivation as the group size increases.

3 A group leader may emerge by prescription, or be elected by external factors or emerge from within the group through peer support.

4 Factors that would make a situation more favourable for a leader are good relationships between leader and group, a clear and easy to understand task, a leader who has authority and respect.

Exam practice

1 Leadership qualities that are important in a sports coach are: they must be well motivated, have a vision or set goal, be a good communicator, show empathy and respect for the group members, be a skilful performer, have a good knowledge of their sport, have a natural talent for leadership.

2 An autocratic style is task-orientated and didactic. It is best in dangerous situations and with larger groups. A democratic style is person-orientated, with the emphasis on human relations and on encouraging others to participate in decision making. It works best in small groups or with individuals and with highly skilled groups.

> **Examiner's secrets**
>
> It is often easier to give practical examples first before using the technical jargon.

Mental preparation for sport

Checkpoints

1 Three examples of typical stressors are competition, conflict and frustrations.

2 An example of self-efficacy in sport is athletes showing a large degree of self-confidence.

3 A coach can utilise knowledge of the inverted U theory of arousal by recognising that every individual member of the team has a different optimum level of performance and may need different means of reaching this level.

4 Trait anxiety is an enduring tendency to exhibit anxiety and state anxiety is the anxiety actually experienced in a particular situation.

Exam practice

1 Somatic anxiety is the physiological effect of stress, manifest in a rise in heart rate and higher adrenaline levels. Cognitive anxiety is the psychological effect manifest as high irritability and a feeling of apprehension.

2 Cognitive techniques of stress management are: imagery, positive thinking, selective attention or mental rehearsal.

Effects and consequences of competition

Checkpoints

1 Social facilitation is the influence other people can have on an individual's performance.

2 The instinct theory suggests that aggression is an innate biological drive and sport simply gives an outlet for this aggression. The frustration–aggression hypothesis is a version of the drive theory which states that blocking goals can cause frustration which then leads to aggression. The social learning theory developed by Bandura states that we learn to be aggressive by watching others.

3 Past experiences/failures which lead a performer to believe that failure is inevitable and the belief that failure is due to uncontrollable factors can create learned helplessness.

4 Learned helplessness can be changed into a positive attribute by retraining to give success, reinforcing good performance and offering positive feedback. These all help to attribute success to stable controllable factors.

Exam practice

An audience may have a positive effect on the performance of gross- or simple-skill, group or low-organisation activities. The more highly skilled or experienced the athlete, the more positive the effect. An audience may have a negative effect on fine- or complex-skill or individual activities that require concentration and focus. This will be magnified if the performer is a beginner, inexperienced or novice.

Revision checklist
Sports psychology

By the end of this chapter you should be able to:		
1 Discuss the different personality types and theories.	Confident	Not confident **Revise** pages 82–83
2 Discuss the difference between introvert and extrovert personalities.	Confident	Not confident **Revise** page 82
3 Explain the differences between intrinsic and extrinsic motivation.	Confident	Not confident **Revise** page 83
4 Explain the differences between *Nach* and *Naf* athletes.	Confident	Not confident **Revise** page 83
5 Explain what factors can affect group cohesion in sport.	Confident	Not confident **Revise** pages 84–85
6 Understand the application of the theories of group dynamics in sport.	Confident	Not confident **Revise** pages 84–85
7 Describe what is meant by the term social loafing.	Confident	Not confident **Revise** page 84
8 Explain the different types of leadership styles.	Confident	Not confident **Revise** page 85
9 Describe how motivation can be affected by the level of self-confidence.	Confident	Not confident **Revise** page 86
10 Outline the theory of goal setting and the use of the SMARTER principles.	Confident	Not confident **Revise** page 86
11 Explain the inverted U theory and its application to sport.	Confident	Not confident **Revise** page 87
12 Describe how athletes can measure and manage stress.	Confident	Not confident **Revise** page 87
13 Discuss the concept of social facilitation and audience effect on sports performance.	Confident	Not confident **Revise** page 88
14 Explain the theories and application of the concept of aggression in sport.	Confident	Not confident **Revise** page 88
15 Discuss the practical application of attribution theory to sport.	Confident	Not confident **Revise** page 89
16 Explain what can create learned helplessness and suggest ways learned helplessness can be changed into a positive attribute.	Confident	Not confident **Revise** page 89

Historical study of physical education and sport

This chapter includes the study of the historical development of sport, reviews the development on society and its effect on sport over the last 500 years. The initial phase of the development of sport was in pre-industrial Britain where different sports were followed by peasant and court. Many of these activities were the origins of our modern sports.

The next stage of development occurred in the great public schools at the start of the nineteenth century. Here boys adopted the old games, refining them into more formal and regular activities. On leaving school the old boys began to transport their love of games around Britain and the British Empire.

The Industrial Revolution changed the way people worked and lived and consequently had a major impact on sport. Most people were now living in towns and cities, with less space for sport, and sports had to be adapted to suit the new urban conditions. Changes in working patterns led to all people having more time for leisure and a more regular style of sport developed.

The final phase of development saw the emergence of physical education in state schools at the start of the twentieth century.

Exam themes

- Development of popular recreation in the UK pre-1800

- The games and festivals of pre-industrial Britain

- The development of sport in the English public schools

- The impact athleticism had on wider society

- The spread of British sports around the world

- The role of the universities in developing sport

- Rational recreation in an urban industrial society

- The need for the codification and organisation of sport in the nineteenth century

- The development of PE in British state schools

- The further development of sport in the twentieth and twenty-first centuries

Topic checklist

	Edexcel		AQA		OCR		WJEC	
	AS	A2	AS	A2	AS	A2	AS	A2
Sport before 1800	○					●		
Sport in the English public schools	○		○			●	○	
The impact of athleticism on society	○		○			●	○	
Sport after 1800 – the rational phase	○		○			●	○	
The development of PE in British state schools 1870–1944	○		○			●	○	

Sport before 1800

The historical development of sport moves through four main phases and questions will either focus on a particular period or ask you to compare developments between phases.

1 **Popular recreation**	fifteenth to seventeenth century
2 **Public school**	eighteenth to nineteenth century
3 **Rationalisation and industrialisation**	nineteenth century
4 **Twentieth century developments** (PE)	twentieth century

Overview of sport before 1800s

In the Middle Ages, the UK's population was almost totally rural. London (the only substantial town in the twelfth century) had a population of only 20,000. There were 30 'holy' days in a year (as well as Sundays) when sports could be played.

The population was split into two main groups: the gentry and the peasants.

For the gentry, the amount of time available, economic and social advantage, and the need to demonstrate their military preparedness made the sporting activities of the ruling classes different from those of the peasants. Key sports were jousting for knights and sports such as real tennis that required sophisticated courts and equipment.

The time available for the peasants to play sport was often restricted to the holy days. They also had less access to resources and travel, so their recreations had to be localised and use ready-to-hand materials. Recreations changed through the year. In the winter, mass, violent games such as mob football were played; in the summer, gentler, more individual and athletic-type activities were followed. The games were often violent contests with few rules.

Take note

It is important that you get your dates right:

1600s seventeenth century Pre-industrial
1700s eighteenth century Pre- into industrial
1800s nineteenth century Industrial
1900s twentieth century Post-industrial
2000s twenty-first century Technological

The jargon

Holy day – a religious festival, which gave the people a day off from work. The usual Christian festivals and local saints days were often used for recreation.

Grade booster

Make sure you recognise the importance of combat sports and their link to the knights and war preparation.

Checkpoint 1

Explain how real tennis was sophisticated in its make-up.

Checkpoint 2

At what time of year were violent mob-type games usually played?

Checkpoint 3

Why were combat sports so popular in pre-industrial society?

Take note

Characteristics of popular recreation:

P re-1800
L ocalised
U ncoded
C ruel
I ndustrial
C ourtly/popular
R ural
O ccasional
W ager

Role of the Church

The year began with the spring fertility festivals, although some games took place as early as New Year's Day and Plough Monday (first Monday after Christmas). Most, however, focussed on Easter. Shrove Tuesday was a particularly popular day for violent mob games (football, tug of war and animal baiting), before the denials of Lent. May Day was often marked by games in which young men chased women (concerned with rituals of fertility). Whitsuntide was the high point of the sporting year with much dancing and games. This was a slack time for agriculture, and crops and animals were left to grow! Summer games tended to be gentler – running, jumping and throwing contests. The Church also provided space to play and would often offer patronage to games and festivals, perhaps providing prizes.

Checkpoint 4

How did the agricultural year affect the time available for sport?

Grade booster

Research at least three examples of popular recreations. Refer to these examples in your answer.

Exam practice   answers: page 104

Sport in the UK before 1800 was closely associated with the Church calendar of holy days and wakes.

1   Why were these days so important for the development of sport?

(6 minutes)

2   Outline the main characteristics of pre-industrial festival games.

(6 minutes)

Sport in the English public schools

In the public schools of the upper classes organised games began to appear, at first as spontaneous recreations and, for the most part, disapproved of by the teachers. However, as they became more developed, it was recognised that educational objectives could be passed on through participation in games.

Sports became a feature of all public schools with team games forming the central core, particularly football and cricket (and rowing at the schools situated near a river). These games were physically strenuous, demanding and relied on cooperation and leadership – all characteristics that a gentleman needed to acquire.

Checkpoint 1

Why were games given so much importance in the public schools?

The three stages of development of the games cult

The change in attitude to sports and games in public schools during the nineteenth century is best viewed as a three-stage progression:

1 The barbarian phase 1790–1830
2 The Arnoldian/athleticism phase
3 The games cult and philistine copies.

The barbarian phase

During this period, schools were unruly places, and there was a constant battle between staff and pupils for control. Boys would bring to school the games and recreations they had taken part in at home. These would have included mob games (various forms of football and stick and ball games), which were mainly spontaneous and very violent. Animal sports were also popular – either hunting or baiting/fighting sports.

The Arnoldian/athleticism phase

In 1827, Dr Thomas Arnold became headmaster of Rugby School, and he was to have an important influence on the reform of the public schools. Although Arnold's main concern was with the education and control of his pupils, the programmes and rules he introduced had a parallel effect on the reform of games and sports in schools.

His main innovations were to introduce:

→ **The house system**, which neatly led to the formation of early sports team prefects who would organise the games and activities of the boys – the first administrators.
→ **Bounds**, whereby games and fights were confined to the school's grounds.
→ **Muscular Christianity** – the idea that there is a close link between Christianity and the concept of sportsmanship.
→ **Philosophy of character** – games were soon seen as a vehicle for developing character.

The games cult and philistine copies

The success of schools such as Rugby led to the cult of games spreading throughout the private education system. The Industrial Revolution was now in full swing, creating a new affluent middle class which provided a huge market for private education. Middle-class families wanted their sons to be educated as gentlemen and to service this need there was a huge growth of preparatory schools. The prominence of games and sports was further enhanced by the publication of the Clarendon Commission report in 1864. Its role was to investigate the management and programmes of the nine great public schools.

The Clarendon Committee 1864

The Committee's main finding was that these schools instilled character in their pupils, many of whom went on to become influential leaders in all walks of life both in Britain and around the Empire. The Commission stated that the system of team games followed by these schools was the main developer of character. Football, in particular, was singled out as encouraging stamina, courage and the ability to withstand knocks.

Checkpoint 2

How did Arnold change the way sports were organised and controlled in the public schools?

The captain of the eleven; what a post is his in our school world; almost as hard as the Doctor's; requiring skill, gentleness and firmness, and I know not what other rare qualities.

Tom Brown's School Days

Checkpoint 3

Why were so many new schools built and opened in the second half of the nineteenth century?

Checkpoint 4

Why was it difficult for schools to play each other at sport during the early nineteenth century?

Checkpoint 5

How did the Clarendon Commission promote the games cult?

Exam practice   answers: page 104

What features of the nineteenth-century schools facilitated regular sports competition?   (8 minutes)

The impact of athleticism on society

The emergence of a modern form of sport through the public school system of the nineteenth century was to have a profound effect on the spread of sport throughout society, both in Britain and throughout the British Empire. It sowed the seeds of the rationalisation of sport, in which sports were codified and regulated by governing bodies, and the boys who left the schools spread the cult of manly games across the world.

Checkpoint 1

What is meant by the term 'sport followed the flag'?

Exploring the games ethic

The missionaries, ambassadors, generals and businessmen initially used games for their own recreation but then began to pass them onto the indigenous peoples of the colonies and other trading nations. The philosophy was to develop some of the moral characteristics that were so important to the English gentleman. Central to this philosophy were team games, as these proved to be the perfect medium for transferring the favourable virtues that made up the games cult.

Through these sports, the indigenous people could learn the basic tools of imperial command: courage, endurance, discipline, loyalty and obedience. Cricket supplied a new conception of chivalry that seemed to reflect exactly the national characteristics of Victorian England. Rugby and football promoted values more suited to imperialism: fearlessness and self-control. In summary, the games developed and promoted by the public schools could produce both the confidence to lead among the ex-pat British and the compulsion to follow among the indigenous people.

Imperialism was felt by most people in Britain to be a very worthwhile, Christian activity. They were moralising and civilising the world – with sport an essential element of this. There were also more sound political reasons for the creation and maintenance of the Empire: trade, security, emigration, prestige and, in the case of Australia, somewhere to dump any criminals or social misfits.

If we ask what our Muscular Christianity has done – we point to the British Empire.

JGC Minchin, 1889

Public school sport travels the world

An effective way of summarising this impact is CAT PUICCA.

C – colonial Many public-school boys took up posts in the colonial service, helping to administer and govern the Empire's many colonies. They took with them their sporting kit. Initially, they played among themselves but gradually introduced the sports and games to the indigenous populations.

A – army Another career for many public-school boys was as commissioned officers in the armed forces. Initially, the officers would use sports as a recreation to fill in long hours, but the social control and moral value of keeping the working-class soldiers occupied were not lost on them. This played an important part in spreading the cult still further.

T – teaching Many former pupils became teachers, especially in the new expanding preparatory and grammar schools. Often, they simply repeated the programme of games and physical recreation they had followed in their schooldays. It was not unusual for sporty teachers to play for the school teams at the end of the nineteenth century.

P – patronage Supporting sporting events and competitions by providing funding for trophies or land for pitches (and in other ways) was another important role undertaken by old boys.

U – university This was a very important stage. Cambridge and Oxford chiefly gave young men further time and resources to pursue and refine sporting activities. One major problem though was the plethora of different rules for the various games. In order to allow all to play, compromise rules were required and this was the first step towards the rationalisation of sport.

I – industry Once they had finished school, many boys returned to their fathers' factories and businesses. These were Arnold's 'philistines'. Their love of sport needed an outlet and soon clubs linked to these factories were set up. At first, there were some social limits – only managers and office staff could join the teams – but gradually the lower classes were also admitted. Many current football teams – Stoke City, West Ham, Manchester United – were formed in this way.

C – Church Much of the boys' education was religion based, so it is not surprising that many boys took up careers in the Church. Muscular Christianity promoted the use of sport as a vehicle for teaching morals and Christian virtues. Many clergymen used it in its most practical form, encouraging sports and setting up teams both here and abroad. Again there are examples in modern football – Aston Villa, Everton and Wolverhampton Wanderers have Church origins.

C – clubs The first stage for many old boys was to form clubs so they could continue to play their games. The Old Etonians is a good example of this type of club, but many more were also formed.

A – administration When their playing days were over, many men joined and developed governing bodies for their sports, and helped to formulate national rules.

Checkpoint 2

Why were the universities of Cambridge and Oxford known as the 'melting pots' of sports?

Take note

The Oxford and Cambridge Boat Race, created in 1829, is one of the oldest sporting events in the world.

Exam practice   answers: page 104

What role did Oxford and Cambridge play in the development of sport during the nineteenth century?   (8 minutes)

Sport after 1800 – the rational phase

The jargon

Codification – the creation and maintenance of rules.

The phase referred to as the rationalisation of sport saw the codification and administration of sport. After the Industrial Revolution, most people lived and worked in urban areas and the influence of the rural elements from the popular recreation era steadily declined. Modern sport is also urban sport.

Societal determinants – societal change that led to rational recreation

→ **Urbanisation** – Large population requiring recreative space and entertainment
→ **Industrialisation** – Factory system and machine time
→ **Work conditions** – Gradual increase in free time, Saturday half-day, Ten Hour Act, Early Closing Movement.
→ **Economics** – Capitalism and patronage, works teams – professional clubs.

Time for sport was governed by social class, and the working classes had to wait much longer for free time than the middle and upper classes. The development of transport allowed inter-town sport competitions and opened up the countryside. Urbanisation meant that only a few people could play, leading to spectatorism and inevitably professionalism. Rational sport became characterised by channelled aggression, stringent organisation, formal rules and regular play. The Factory Acts of the late nineteenth century finally gave working-class people more leisure time, with most being given Saturday afternoons off work.

Checkpoint 1

What effect did urbanisation and industrialisation have on sport during the nineteenth century?

Checkpoint 2

How did the half-day acts facilitate the development of sport at the end of the nineteenth century?

Working-class people tended to be drawn to sports that could make money – lack of leisure time meant that playing sport often meant the loss of wages, a situation few working people could afford. This led to football and rugby teams paying players 'broken-time payments', a development that caused much ill feeling between the classes and led to a further division – a north–south divide (clubs in the north tended to be more open towards paying working-class players). Towards the end of the nineteenth century, this led to the development of professionalism in many sports.

Initially, fixtures among clubs were rather ad hoc affairs. Gentlemen's clubs would arrange fixtures on a day and date that suited both parties, and most of these amateur players had no constraints on when and where they could play. The rules played to were also rather informal – games could change at half-time from football rules to rugby rules. Generally, the home team chose the particular rule and the away team provided the ball – but this did not always work in harmony.

As more and more teams became active, this ad hoc arrangement had to change. Clubs began to meet and form associations in order to make matches more regular and to reach a compromise over the rules of play. Such meetings ultimately led to the formation of national governing bodies in all major sports by the end of the nineteenth century.

The jargon

Broken-time payments – clubs paid working-class players the wages they could not earn while playing.

Checkpoint 3

How had the relationship between spectators and performers changed by the end of the nineteenth century?

Checkpoint 4

What changes in sport led to the need for governing bodies at the end of the nineteenth century?

Grade booster

You may be asked to compare the characteristics of popular and rational recreation. Draw a table and use the mnemonic PLUCI CROW as a start point. Look for opposites to summarise sport in the rational phase.

Exam practice   answers: page 104

Explain the effect that both the transport and urban revolutions had on the organisation of rational sport at the start of the twentieth century.

(10 minutes)

The development of PE in British state schools

Modern PE grew from two main pathways: games from the public schools, which aimed to develop character and leadership, and physical training from elementary schools, devised to develop fitness and discipline. The 1870 Forster Act made education compulsory, but there was limited development of PE due to the lack of facilities and space.

Early forms of physical education

There were two main influences on this gymnastic development, stemming from two different European countries:

→ **German** – based on the work of Johann Guts Muths and Friedrich Ludwig Jahn
→ **Swedish** – based on the work of Per Henrik Ling.

It was the Swedish system of 'drill', inspired by Ling, that had the biggest impact on the development of physical education in Britain. Using the German system as his inspiration, Ling simplified the exercises and reduced the military bias, concentrating more on style and grace. He also paid respect to the classical tradition, emphasising the harmony between body and mind. Ling's system was adopted by many school boards in Britain – most importantly, the London School Board, who appointed Madame Bergman Osterberg to oversee this implementation. She played a central role in the development of PE in Britain, establishing the first specialist teacher-training college at Dartford in 1895.

The model course

The first model course for physical education in schools was written by the War Office in 1902, prompted by the poor health of recruits for the Boer War. This syllabus was revised with a different focus in 1904–19, and a modern syllabus, taking the best of physical training and introducing PE as a subject in schools, was introduced in 1933.

Key developments

→ **nineteenth century** – European roots *Ling and Guts Muths*
→ **1870** – Forster Education Act. *Made education compulsory for all children 5–13*
→ **1902** – Model course. *Compulsory military training in schools required to lay the foundations of military spirit in the nation*
→ **1904** – Education Board syllabus. *An attempt to reduce the military influence*
→ **1909** – Syllabus of Physical Training. *Written by Medical Board – emphasis on therapeutic gymnastics*
→ **1919** – Syllabus. *Reflecting the horrors of the Great War – introduced recreational and morale-boosting activities*
→ **1933** – Syllabus of Physical Training. *Last Board of Education syllabus split into two sections 5–11 years and 11–14 years*

Checkpoint 1

Why was there only a limited development of PE in state schools prior to 1870?

Take note

The 1870 Education Act set up Education Boards, funded in part through rates, to establish primary education.

Take note

Physical education developed through stages: drill → physical training → physical education.

Checkpoint 2

What role did Madame Bergman Osterberg play in the development of physical education in the UK?

Checkpoint 3

Who was responsible for writing the model course and what was the resulting bias?

1870–1944

→ **1944 – Education Act.** *Made secondary education available to all children – rebuilding of schools after the blitz*

→ **1952 – *Moving and Growing*.** *Ministry of Education advisory PE publication followed by* Planning the Programe (1954).

PE after 1945

Post-war educational philosophy led to a movement away from prescribed syllabuses and in 1952 the Ministry of Education published *Moving and Growing* and in 1954 *Planning the Programme*. All PE teachers received copies. These publications offered advice and suggestions rather than commands, and represented the final move towards a child-centred approach to physical education.

Sport in the twentieth century

Several factors have affected the development of sport through the twentieth century. There was a steady move away from participation in sport to the phenomenon of watching sport, initially through spectatorism but increasingly through the media. Spectatorism generated money, which led to professionalism in virtually all sports. Many sports performers are now full-time paid entertainers.

The development of television greatly expanded the potential sports audience and made sport even more attractive to commercial sponsors. By the end of the century, satellite broadcasting had turned sport into a global activity.

Sport in the twenty-first century

Sport, with its related services, is now the biggest employer in the world. It attracts the largest audiences of any activity on the planet. Sports goods and performers have developed into the best known and most powerful global brands, elite performers are now multi millionaires and now endorse and advertise a whole array of household products and services.

Because sport is so popular, sports events can demand the highest media rights, with TV channels willing to spend huge amounts in return for exclusive broadcasting rights. The funding the media companies plough into sport also means that they now wield significant power in dictating when and where global sports events take place. The now ubiquitous satellite coverage of sports events means that players, teams and leagues are now looking at global markets. Football matches in England kick off at times that suit the massive TV audiences in Asia, sports like baseball now open their seasons with games in Japan and most Premiership football teams now go on a pre-season tour to the Far East – all in the name of replica shirt sales. The next step is the globalisation of league teams from several countries playing each other in cross-border competitions. To some extent, this already exists in soccer with the hugely popular and financially lucrative UEFA Champions League and in rugby with the Super 12 competition amongst southern hemisphere club teams.

> **Checkpoint 4**
>
> How did *Moving and Growing*, published in 1952, differ from earlier syllabuses?

> **Grade booster**
>
> There is a lot to cover here, make sure you have a good knowledge of the key developments and don't forget to write about the influence of war.

> **Exam practice** answers: page 105
>
> How did war influence the early development of physical education in British state schools at the beginning of the twentieth century? (8 minutes)

Answers
Historical study of physical education and sport

Sport before 1800

Checkpoints

1 Real tennis was a sophisticated game. It required a purpose-built court, the equipment was handmade and had no other use than playing tennis. The scoring system of the game required education and a basic knowledge of arithmetic.
2 Mob-type games tended to be played during the winter, when there was a need to move and keep warm and when there were no problems over using the field as pitches.
3 Combat sports were popular in pre-industrial society because of the need to be fit for war. They also offered a chance for gambling and entertainment and were easily accessible for all classes.
4 The agricultural year governed how much spare time the people had. Spring and autumn were busy times with little time for sports, whereas in winter and summer there was more time.

Exam practice

1 Holy days and wakes were important for the development of sport because these were the only days free from work when large groups of the community could come together. Patronage by the Church was in the form of providing land for games and prizes.
2 The main characteristics of pre-industrial festival games were the use of large spaces, and games in the form of rural activities. They were only played once a year/occasionally, were only played in a particular place and the lack of transport meant that games were localised. Games had few rules, were often violent, and involved large numbers of participants. There was a loose distinction between participants and spectators.

Sport in the English public schools

Checkpoints

1 Games were given much importance in the public school system. Games developed character and reinforced many of the values, such as leadership and honour, that a gentlemen was meant to possess. They were also an effective means of social control.
2 Arnold gave responsibility for organising sports to the prefects and sixth-formers.
3 Many new schools were built and opened in the second half of the nineteenth century because the expanding middle class meant that there was a demand to send sons and daughters to private or preparatory schools.
4 The difficulty for schools wanting to play each other was that transport was still a limiting factor, so the main focus for competition was house matches.
5 The Clarendon Commission reported that the best schools in the UK all had extensive systems of school sport.

Exam practice

Features of the nineteenth-century schools that facilitated regular sports competition were:
The house structure of the boarding schools gave a natural focus for competition, there was also support from headmasters and they allowed time after lessons for the boys to play. Control by the upper school gave a certain degree of peer pressure.

The impact of athleticism on society

Checkpoints

1 In sport, the term 'followed the flag' refers to the way in which sports that originated in Britain quickly spread across the rest of the world, especially where the British colonial influence was strong.
2 Melting pot refers to the fact that undergraduates brought various rules of games from the many public schools to the universities, which were the first place where an attempt at creating compromise rules occurred.

Exam practice

Oxford and Cambridge university acted as a melting pot for the mixing of the numerous versions of sports rules arriving from the schools.

Sport after 1800 – the rational phase

Checkpoints

1 Urbanisation meant a lack of space for sport, and industrialisation changed the calendar and meant there was less time for sport.
2 The half-day acts gave working-class people time to take up sport, so increasing the participation rates.
3 There was now a clear distinction between spectators and players. Pitch markings and stadia now kept them well apart.
4 By the end of the nineteenth century, transport had developed, which allowed teams and individuals to travel, so there was now a need for national sets of rules and bodies to organise fixtures and competitions.

Exam practice

The transport revolution meant that teams could travel to play one another, which led to a need for national sets of rules and the formation of governing bodies. This also meant that national leagues and competitions could be set up. Urbanisation meant there was less space to play sport and that pitches had to be formalised. It also led to the rise in spectatorism since large numbers could no longer play sport.

The development of PE in British state schools 1870–1944

Checkpoints

1 There was limited development of PE in state schools prior to 1870 because schooling was not compulsory before 1870, so very few working-class children would have attended.
2 Madame Bergman Osterberg played a central role in the development of PE in Britain. She introduced a system of Swedish drill to schools in London and set up the first training college for PE teachers.
3 The War Office produced the model course and this resulted in a very military approach, treating pupils as little soldiers.
4 *Moving and Growing* only offered guidance and suggestions; there was no compulsion or prescription.

Exam practice

The need for a fit and obedient working-class army affected the scope and provision of PE. The failings of the Boer War led to the introduction of the model course, written and produced by the War Office. This course was taught by NCOs. The First World War led to a re-emphasis on drill, though the role that sports and games had played in the convalescence camps was acknowledged. The Second World War led to a more child-centred approach, mirroring the change in military tactics and also the rebuilding of schools with sports facilities.

Revision checklist
Historical study of physical education and sport

By the end of this chapter you should be able to:

1	Outline the development of popular recreation in the UK pre-1800.	Confident	Not confident. **Revise** pages 94–95
2	Explain the importance of combat sports and their link to the knights and war preparation in pre-industrial society.	Confident	Not confident. **Revise** page 94
3	Give examples of and describe the games and festivals of pre-industrial Britain.	Confident	Not confident. **Revise** pages 94–95
4	Trace the development of sport in the English public schools.	Confident	Not confident. **Revise** pages 96–97
5	Explain the role of the universities in developing sport during the nineteenth century.	Confident	Not confident. **Revise** page 99
6	Describe the effect urbanisation and industrialisation had on sport during the nineteenth century.	Confident	Not confident. **Revise** pages 100–101
7	Describe how the half-day acts facilitated the development of sport at the end of the nineteenth century.	Confident	Not confident. **Revise** page 100
8	Explain the changes in sport that led to the need for governing bodies at the end of the nineteenth century.	Confident	Not confident. **Revise** page 101
9	Discuss how physical education developed through stages: drill → physical training → physical education.	Confident	Not confident. **Revise** pages 102–103
10	Explain the structure of and need for the model course introduced in 1902.	Confident	Not confident. **Revise** page 102

The comparative study of global sporting systems

The key to understanding comparative study is to recognise that sport reflects the culture in which it is being played. Socio-cultural difference will have an effect on the way sport is organised and provided, and opportunities to participate may differ between cultures. Some examination boards require students to undertake a comparative analysis of sport using the UK as the base culture so it may be worth reviewing the material covered in the seventh chapter of this guide.

For each culture, we will investigate the socio-cultural background then trace the historical development of sport and discuss how sport is organised now. We also need to investigate the role that physical education and school sport play in the society and contrast élite and mass sport.

Exam themes

- Overview of sport in the USA
- The administration of sport in the USA
- Historical development of sport and PE in the USA
- Mass participation and élite sport in the USA
- Culture and background of Australian sport
- Overview of sport in Australia
- Historical development of Australian sport and PE
- The administration of sport in Australia
- School and college sport in Australia
- Mass participation and élite sport in Australia

Topic checklist

	Edexcel		AQA		OCR		WJEC	
	AS	A2	AS	A2	AS	A2	AS	A2
Sport in North American cultures		●		●		●		●
Administration of sport in North American cultures		●		●		●		●
Mass participation and élite sport in the USA		●		●		●		●
Sport in New World culture – Australia		●				●		
Administration of sport in Australia		●				●		●
Mass participation and élite sport in Australia		●				●		●

Sport in North American cultures

America's major sports are not really played anywhere else in the world – this is a good example of sport reflecting the culture of a society. America's history and self-belief have established a sports system where it can hold 'world championships' in American football, baseball, basketball and ice hockey in which only American teams compete.

The jargon

Lombardian ethic – named after the famous Green Bay Packers' most successful coach, Vince Lombardi, who developed the idea that winning is the most important thing.

The jargon

American Dream – the idea that in the USA anyone can rise from rags to riches.

Checkpoint 1

Explain how the rags to riches ideal can be achieved through sport in the USA.

Checkpoint 2

Sport in the USA is dominated by the private sector. What forms of funding are available to US sports?

Checkpoint 3

What is meant by the term 'endorsement'?

Overview

→ Sports are the most technically advanced in the world
→ Sports stars are the richest in the world
→ Sports-mad public – large audiences
→ World champions in a number of sports
→ Americanisation spreading throughout global sport.

America's sports tend to be high scoring and action packed to maximise their entertainment value. They reflect American culture in that the aim is to win – the win ethic, or Lombardian ethic, is what drives all American people and this fuels the 'American Dream'. (This idea of 'rags to riches' success is best personified in the 'Rocky' films, where a nobody becomes world champion overnight.)

The commercial aspect of American sport makes it unique. Every level, from professional national teams to the local high-school football team, is run as a business. The influence of television is total and most sports rely on the money generated through television deals and advertising revenue. Many sports stars in America are millionaires – indeed, most professional teams will have a number of players on multi-million-dollar contracts. Many stars, such as Michael Jordan, make even more money through sponsorship deals and endorsements.

The historical development of sport in North American cultures

	Historical phase of development	Sports phase of development	Sports example
1	Heritage of ancient civilisations	Ancient Games	Baggataway/ Lacrosse
2	Arrival of the Europeans	Arrival of the Europeans	Baseball
3	Rationalisation phase	Rationalisation phase	American football
4	New image and isolation and ethnic melting pot	New image and isolation	Basketball
5	Superpower	Sport the commodity	Extreme sports

The USA was once a colony of Great Britain, but this link was severed early in the country's development and for many years the USA developed in planned isolation from the rest of the world, and in particular Europe. During this period, many of America's sports were adapted from old European games to suit America's new image. In sports such as football and hockey, a more robust, glamorous version has developed and distinctive American sports (such as basketball) were invented on American soil. So closely did these sports mirror American society that they have never really developed away from America's shores.

The commercial nature of American sport

Every level, from professional teams to the local high-school football team, is run as a business. The influence of the media is total and most of the national sports in North America rely on money generated through television deals and advertising revenue. Television has so much power in American sport that it can even dictate a sport's rules. American football, for example, has evolved into a game with many stoppages so that TV companies can screen advertisements every five minutes. Sports stars in America become millionaires from their playing contracts and can earn much more money through sponsorship deals and endorsements.

This commercial nature means that sport in America is extremely élitist and there are very few amateur clubs or opportunities for people of lower ability to access sport. Nearly all of America's sports clubs are based in educational establishments such as schools and colleges or professional enterprises. This means that for most Americans, sport is something you watch on television and is not something most people play after leaving school.

Checkpoint 4

How does American football reflect the culture of the USA?

The jargon

Endorsement – where a sports star is paid to put their name into the sale of a product or a commodity.

Grade booster

Be able to use specific examples from US sports in your answers. Research some of the teams that play in the professional leagues. Find out who are the stars of US sport.

Exam practice   answers: page 120

Give historical and cultural reasons to explain the fact that the USA holds 'world championships' in sports which only American teams compete in.

(8 minutes)

Administration of sport in North American cultures

There is a decentralised administration with autonomous governing bodies in North American culture. There are a small number of powerful professional sports with considerable public support, run as profit-making businesses through the franchise system. There is much commercial sponsorship and major media influence – the private sector is the main source of funding. The Lomabardian 'win at all costs' ethic dominates all American sport and is reflected in the link between professionalism and capitalism, although there is a strong and growing counterculture movement linking the rise of lifetime sport and eco sport. The college system acts as a sponsored nursery for professional and Olympic sport. There are limited opportunities for amateur sport and few public facilities.

Checkpoint 1

What is meant by the term 'autonomous'?

School and college sport

School and college sport in the USA is unique. In sparsely populated areas or less well-off areas, where long distances must be travelled to watch one of the professional National League teams, the school or college team becomes a substitute for community attention.

The jargon

Booster clubs – community clubs made up of old boys and local businessmen who gave financial support to school and college teams.

Sport in high schools – key points

→ High-school sports form a link between education and professional sports
→ High-school sports are a microcosm of professional games
→ Most high schools possess lavish facilities for sports
→ School sports are followed by the community
→ School sports are funded by booster clubs.

High-school sports link the education system and professional sports industries.

Checkpoint 2

What role do booster clubs play in the financing and promotion of school and college sport?

Checkpoint 3

What does Title IX legislate against?

High-school Team

↓

College Scholarship

↓

Draft

↓

Professional League

School and college sport is the main route to a career in sport. A unique feature of this system is recruitment through school–college–professional leagues. The system is very élitist, however, with only 3 per cent moving from school to college teams and in basketball only 1 in 10,000 getting into draft. Coaches and scouts working for the college visit high schools across the country, identifying and attempting to recruit players to come and play for their team. To attract players they emphasise the quality of their facilities, the chances of playing in a successful team and therefore a better chance of making the 'draft' – and, of course, the 'athletic scholarship'.

The draft system

This acts as the bridge between the college system and professional leagues. The draft system, together with salary capping, ensures that teams are not able simply to buy their way to success.

In the draft system, teams in each of the major professional sports are ranked at the end of each season, as are the outstanding college players likely to arouse the interest of professional clubs. The lowest-ranked club has the first choice of the highest-ranked player so that, theoretically at least, some form of parity is maintained.

Intramural sport does exist and is where players of a lower standard play for fun. It is very low profile and often occurs late at night after the college teams have finished training.

The jargon

Athletic scholarships – grant-in-aid to help cover tuition fees and board.

The jargon

Draft system – the system where professional teams select the best college players once a year.

Checkpoint 4

How does the draft system attempt to reflect the American ideal of the land of opportunity?

Exam practice   answers: page 120

Suggest reasons for the huge community interest and support for high-school sport in the USA.   (8 minutes)

Mass participation and élite sport in the USA

American sport has not evolved a sports club system similar to that in northern Europe. Sport tends to be focussed on high school, college and professional franchises. There is only limited opportunity outside these spheres to participate in sports.

Mass participation

Urban parks and other open spaces do offer Americans the chance to jog, skate and play touch football or softball, but generally there is little public-sector sport provision.

One exception is 'little league' sport. This consists of club leagues for children under ten, and run in a number of different sports – Pop Warner football, Pee Wee Baseball and Biddy Basketball are examples.

Teams are run by parents and compete in structured league competitions that mirror the professional leagues, with conferences, play-offs and 'superbowls'. The main emphasis is on winning and this has led to some criticism; however, most Americans support the system because they feel that it helps reinforce in children the American way of life. The current USA President is a former little league baseball player – which has led to the motto: 'from little league to White House'.

As we have previously discussed, the ethic of sport in America has been replaced by spectatorism, with most Americans happy to watch élite performers play. There has been a recent move towards lifetime sport, mainly to counter problems over increasing levels of obesity among the American population. This move towards participation has been readily taken up by older Americans, with most areas now holding 'golden Olympics'.

Alternative and wilderness sports

The National Parks Service, created in 1916, reflected the aim of America as the land of the free. The combination of cars and a wilderness that is easily accessible gives most Americans the chance to experience the frontier spirit. One of the areas that has increased in popularity is the so-called eco sport. Activities such as skiing, backpacking, white-water rafting and mountain biking have boomed in recent years. These activities are part of a counter-culture, an escape from the élite 'win ethic' culture of most American sport.

Checkpoint 1

Explain what is meant by the term 'professional franchise'.

Checkpoint 2

How does little league sport mirror the professional sports scene of the USA?

The jargon

Lifetime sport – a sport that can be played throughout a person's life.

The jargon

Title IX – made law in 1972, this laid down rights of access to sport for women and girls on an equal basis to men. Equal opportunity had to be provided for facilities, coaching and financial support. If an institution that received federal money failed to provide equal opportunity, then these monies would be withheld.

The jargon

Eco sport – recreational activities with little organisation and natural in focus.

Checkpoint 3

Explain what is meant by the term 'counter-culture'?

Many American children also attend summer camps. These residential activity camps are usually sited well away from cities and towns and often concentrate on outdoor sports and activities. There are thousands of these camps across the states, catering for all pockets and tastes.

Private camps	Very exclusive and expensive, these are often very specialised, catering for specific sports or interests. The more traditional camps still focus on developing a sense of frontier spirit among camp attendees.
Charity and Church camps	Costs are subsidised due to sponsorship from Church or charity groups. These camps tend to offer a range of outdoor activities.
State camps	The state government pays for under-privileged children to attend a summer camp.

Professional and élite sport

Sport in the USA is run through a decentralised system of autonomous governing bodies with little state or federal intervention. A number of powerful professional sports enjoy considerable support from the American public. These sports are run on a franchise basis and are very commercially oriented, with the main priority of all clubs being to make a profit.

The private sector dominates American sport; there is very little voluntary or public-sector provision. Sport relies on gate receipts, media fees and, increasingly, commercial sponsorship.

The jargon

Franchise – a business agreement set up to maximise profit.

Checkpoint 4

Explain the role the media plays in sport in the USA.

Grade booster

Be able to discuss how the structure and philosophy of the US sports system may inhibit participation.

Exam practice   answers: page 120

Suggest why the ethic of mass participation may not sit comfortably in the culture of the USA. (7 minutes)

Sport in New World culture – Australia

Australia has a comparatively small population, yet enjoys an extraordinary degree of success on the sports field. There are few sporting events in which Australia does not excel and statistics show that Australia gains more Olympic gold medals than any other nation.

Cultural background

Australia is a 'young' country, in terms of both its culture and its population – nearly half its population is under the age of 30 (in the UK, 50 per cent of the population is over the age of 50).

It has a relatively small population of only 18 million, and so one would think that it was a sparsely populated country. In some ways, this is true but Australia is also a land of contradictions and is in fact one of the most urbanised populations – 85 per cent of the population lives in only 3.3 per cent of the nation's land area.

Checkpoint 1

Explain how having a 'youthful' population is an advantage in terms of international sporting success.

Australia's people

The original inhabitants of Australia, the Aboriginal people, are one of the oldest civilisations in the world. They arrived in Australia during the Ice Age when Australia was connected to Asia via land bridges. But as it moved away from the Asian continent, Australia and its inhabitants were isolated for several thousands of years, until in the eighteenth century European explorers discovered Terra Australis Incognita ('the unknown southern land').

Historical development

The British established a colony in Australia in 1788. A fleet of 11 vessels containing 736 convicted criminals, a governor, some officials and an escort of Royal Marines founded the colony on the eastern coast of Australia in what later became New South Wales. This was the first European settlement of any kind in Australia, an area that was at the time little known about in Europe.

Transportation was an important part of the British penal system. Convicts had, before this time, been sent to America but now the American Revolution and independence meant that this country could no longer be used. By 1852, 160,000 convicts had been sent to Australia. After the establishment of the first colony, many 'free settlers' also left Britain for Australia. This immigration gained pace in the 1850s when gold was discovered in many areas of south-west Australia. By 1861, there were over 1 million white Australians (compare this with the native population – in 1887 there were only 750,000 Aborigines).

After the First World War, Britain's hold on the colonies began to dwindle and the Balfour Declaration of 1926 and the Statute of Westminster, 1931, conceded control to the colonies and led to the recognition of Australia's states as governments in their own right.

Geography and culture

Though a vast and diverse country, the majority of the Australian people live on the low-lying coastal plains running around the south and east coast. This has a positive impact on sport, as these areas experience a temperate climate which is favourable for sport in the outdoors. It also means that a large percentage of the Australian population lives very close to the thousands of miles of beach and coastline – a free and accessible natural facility for a range of sports. The size and diversity of the country also mean that there are numerous opportunities for a vast range of sports from skiing to surfing.

Checkpoint 2

How did the transportation system aid the development of Australia?

Checkpoint 3

How is Australia's colonial history reflected in the sports they play?

Exam practice answers: page 120

Explain the popularity of outdoor sport and activities both in Australian schools and communities. (8 minutes)

Administration of sport in Australia

Australia consists of a number of self-governing states and two areas that have territorial status. The country is governed under a federal system similar to the one that operates in the USA, the main difference being that Australia has maintained its Commonwealth status and consequently the British queen is still its head of state. The system of administration is decentralised.

Administration of sport

The administration and organisation of sport and recreation in Australia follows this decentralised system, with each state and territory having a department responsible for sport and recreation and its own élite academy of sport. There is, however, another example of a compromise, with a powerful centralising effect from the federally funded Australian Sports Commission and its sports institute network.

Australia is certainly a sports-obsessed nation, with over 120 national sporting organisations and it is estimated that around 6.5 million people, around a third of the population, are registered members of a sporting club.

The role of the Commonwealth government

The Commonwealth or federal government of Australia funds and develops sport and physical activity through the Australian Sports Commission. It also actively supports and funds the hosting of international sports events such as the 2000 Sydney Olympic and Paralympic Games

The role of the state government

There are six separate state governments in Australia and they all take an active role in the promotion and coordination of sport, physical education and active recreation. It is the state sport and recreation department, funded directly by government, that is responsible for implementing Active Australia programmes in their state. Each state also has its own policies and programmes that support both élite sport and mass participation.

The role of local government

Again, this level of government plays an important role in delivering the Active Australia programmes. Local government is in the best position to assist services and distribute funds in the best interests of community groups.

The Australian Sports Commission (ASC) has three main objectives:

1 To develop and maintain an effective national sports infrastructure.
2 To improve participation by Australians in quality sports activities.
3 To encourage excellence in sports performance by Australians.

Checkpoint 1

What is meant by the term 'federal' in the context of governance?

Checkpoint 2

How does being a member of the Commonwealth maintain the link between Australia and the UK?

Example

The state of Victoria, for example, has established a dynamic Active for Life strategy, with its slogan 'Just find thirty minutes a day'.

The jargon

Australian Sports Commission (ASC) – set up in 1885 by the federal government, this is the body responsible for increasing participation and developing sports excellence in Australia.

Each state has its own sport and recreation department which is responsible for promoting sports participation in that state. All states also have their own dynamic élite sports programme focused around an Institute of Sport.

PE and school provision

Physical education is compulsory in all Australian schools, although again there is variation in content and scheduling across the states. The education department in each state is responsible for all educational matters, though in the case of physical education and school sport they will often work closely with the state's department of sport and recreation.

Two programmes dominate sport for young people in Australia:

The Victoria Model

→ 100 minutes of PE a week compulsory.
→ 100 minutes of sport education a week compulsory.
→ All school teams must play in school time.
→ State department runs, funds and organises inter-school sport.

Fundamental Motor Skills programme

→ Identification of key motor skills for adult sports.
→ Fair go for all.
→ Every primary school teacher in Victoria receives a copy.
→ Government schools can access further training free of charge.

Aussie Sport programme

Developed by ASC and set up in 1986, the Aussie Sport programme was designed to overcome the lack of games skills and to increase participation in sport by school-aged children.

Programmes were run at weekends/out of school hours but used school facilities. The key was the introduction of 'mini' games – modified versions of adult games.

Examples of Aussie Sport programmes include:

→ Netta netball
→ Minky hockey
→ Kick-A-Roo soccer
→ Auskick Aussie Rules.

Checkpoint 3

How does the administration of Australia's sport follow a decentralised system?

Checkpoint 4

Who is responsible for the structure and content of PE programmes in Australia?

Checkpoint 5

Explain the aim of the Fundamental Motor Skills programme.

Examiner's secrets

Be able to compare the provision of PE and school sport in Australia with your own experience in UK schools.

Exam practice   answers: page 121

A unique feature of Australian schools is the provision of Sport Education in Physical Education Programs (SEPEP) within the curriculum. Explain the structure and philosophy of the Sport Education in Physical Education Program. (9 minutes)

Mass participation and élite sport in Australia

Federal government figures suggest that 90 per cent of the Australian population actively participates in sports activities and there are 6.5 million registered players in Australia, affiliated to over 30,000 sports clubs. This national framework, issued by the ASC, requires each state government's recreation department to set up and run programmes and campaigns that follow the guidelines and aims set out in the Active Australia policy document.

Mass participation

Checkpoint 1

Outline the aims of the Active Australia programme.

Active Australia is about promoting healthy lifestyles through participation in regular physical activity. Launched in 1997, Active Australia involves a nationwide network of schools and sport, and recreation and fitness clubs, with links to federal, state and local government.

The programme focusses on two main areas:

→ Encouraging people to be more physically active.
→ Working to improve the places where people can be active.

Example

The Australian Sports Commission promotes active recreation for older members of its population through the mature age sport programme.

The state departments of sport and recreation are involved in the actual delivery of Active Australia and, where appropriate, ensure that state-funded programmes share the same objectives.

Outdoor and adventure activities

Australia has a great range of areas of outstanding natural beauty and its modern integrated transport system makes the outback accessible to all Australians, many of whom make use of it at weekends and in holidays. The other main natural resource is the extensive coastline, especially around the main population centres in the south-east. The beach and coast remain the most important recreational facility in the country, and related sports and activities such as surfing, fishing and boating are extremely popular.

Checkpoint 2

Can you identify the natural and cultural advantages Australia may have over the UK in terms of sports participation?

Professional and élite sport

Checkpoint 3

What geographical factors may limit the scope of professional sport in Australia?

Australia followed Britain in its reluctance to accept professionalism in sport – even now, few Australian sports have totally embraced full-time professional status. Many Australian sports stars ply their trade on foreign shores, where the level of reward and chance of exposure are greater. The big two Australian sports – Australian rules football and rugby league – are both fully professional and supported by large audiences (both live and on television), commercial and sponsorship funding, as well as public funding, in the system of state and national sports academies. Professional sports tend to be administered by a hybrid system of British-style governing bodies operating through American-style franchise agreements.

It is in Olympic sport that the Australian system excels. Their preparation of athletes is now being copied by many other nations, including the UK. The formation of the Australian Institute of Sport (AIS) in 1981 was a significant move in terms of the nurturing of sports talent and government involvement in sports administration. The lead-up to the formation of the AIS followed a pattern similar to the one that occurred in France at the same time – failure at the 1976 Montreal Olympics led to a national outcry and spurred the federal government to fund and reorganise élite sport.

The Australian Institute of Sport

Possibly the best centre for élite athlete preparation in the world, this network of sports academies provides Australia's top performers with the best support. The AIS is funded 95 per cent from federal funds and 5 per cent from commercial sponsorship, with Kellogg's currently a major sponsor. Top athletes receive scholarships to attend the AIS – 500 full-time and 270 visiting scholarships are available each year.

The AIS is not simply one centre. Its main base is in the federal capital of Canberra but due to the vastness of Australia, it runs a decentralised programme of outreach centres in each state's capital city.

Examiner's secrets

The institute system is a unique feature of sport in Australia and is a very popular topic for examiners to ask questions about.

Checkpoint 4

How does the structure of the AIS reflect the decentralising factors of the separate states in Australia?

The structure of Australian sport

Australian Institute of Sport

State institutes

Club sport

SEPEP and sport

Sports search

Aussie Sport

Fundamental Motor Skills

Exam practice answers: page 121

Describe some of the strategies that Australia has used in an attempt to establish Olympic success. (10 minutes)

Answers

The comparative study of global sporting systems

Sport in North American cultures

Checkpoints

1 A performer can start playing in a little league and work their way up to the professional ranks and become a millionaire sports star.
2 Funding available for sport in the USA comes from commercial sponsorship, merchandising, media fees, gate receipts and private investors.
3 Endorsement is where a sports star allows a company to use their name on the company's products.
4 American football reflects the culture of the USA in that it is a very sophisticated and technical game with a large division of labour with very specialist positions. It is also high scoring and entertaining.

Exam practice

The USA holds 'world championships' in sports which only Americans compete in because the USA has a long history of independence and had a period of state-led isolation that coincided with the rational phase of sports development. Most sports competitions in the USA developed at this time, and the huge size and variety of states led to a high level of competition. The big four sports in the USA are so far ahead that there is no point in any other nations competing.

Administration of sport in North American cultures

Checkpoints

1 Autonomous means self-governing, independent.
2 Booster clubs are community clubs made up of old boys and local businessmen who provide financial support to school and college teams.
3 Title IX legislates against gender discrimination in sport in USA educational institutions.
4 The draft system attempts to reflect the American ideal of the land of opportunity in that the worst team gets the first pick, so in theory every team at the start of each season should have an equal opportunity to win.

Exam practice

Some reasons for the huge community interest and support for high-school sport in America are: huge distance between professional teams; schools give a place to socialise for US communities; schools act as nurseries for élite sport; stadia and facilities are of a very high standard; school sport is followed by the media.

Mass participation and élite sport in the USA

Checkpoints

1 The term professional franchise means a business agreement set up to maximise profit.

2 Little league competition in the USA mirrors the professional sports scene in that it follows the 'conference and play' model of all professional sports, the equipment and uniforms are scaled-down versions of the adult game, and the underlying ethic is still to win.
3 Counter-culture is one that goes against the mainstream. In the USA, this is manifest in the recreational ethic, that is, taking part is more important than winning.
4 The media funds sport in the USA, controls the timing of sports events, advertises and promotes sports, and increasingly owns sports clubs.

Exam practice

The USA is an élitist society where the drive is to be successful and win. Playing sport at a lower level can be seen as wasting one's energy, which would be better focussed on gaining the American Dream. The decentralised and private-sector-dominated sports scene also means there are few opportunities both in terms of clubs and facilities to participate at local level.

Sport in New World culture – Australia

Checkpoints

1 Having a 'youthful' population is an advantage in terms of international sporting success because it means there is a large pool to select from. Sport is mainly a young person's activity.
2 The transportation system aided the development of Australia because it meant that Britain could quickly populate the new continent and use the prisoners to build the infrastructure.
3 Australia's colonial history is reflected in the sports they play as they tend to play sports that originated in the UK. Australia has really adapted one sport only – Australian rules, from rugby. Recently, immigration from southern Europe has led to an increase in the scope and popularity of soccer.

Exam practice

Outdoor sport in Australia is popular in schools due to the closeness of the outback to most population centres and the need to teach young people about the dangers and survival techniques. Outdoor pursuits are also a good way of using a free resource around most schools.

Outdoor sport is popular among Australian communities due to the accessibility of the outback and beach. The temperate weather suits outdoor activity and also reflects on the pioneering tradition of the country.

> **Grade booster**
>
> This question requires you to answer two parts, one regarding schools and one part regarding communities. If you want to score high marks you will need to answer both parts.

Administration of sport in Australia

Checkpoints

1 The term federal, in the context of governance, relates to the national or commonwealth government. Australia also has separate state governments.

2 Being a member of the Commonwealth maintains a link between Australia and the UK because the queen remains the head of state and there are still close links between the two governments. It also allows both countries to compete in the Commonwealth Games.

3 Australia's sport follows a decentralised system. Each state has its own independent department of sport and recreation that takes responsibility for all levels of sport in their state. The ASC does attempt to coordinate sports policy across Australia.

4 Each state is responsible for the structure and content of PE programmes in Australia and has its own education department which works closely with the state department of sport and recreation to coordinate PE programmes across their own state.

5 The Fundamental Motor Skills programme's aims are the identification of key motor skills for adult sports. These are taught to all school pupils in order to give a 'fair go for all' in sport.

Exam practice

The structure and philosophy of the Sports Education in Physical Education Program includes: compulsory sports lessons for all separate from PE to give all pupils a chance to participate in sport on a regular basis; a season of sport runs in each term based on internal competition; students run the sessions – coaching and officiating, giving an opportunity to take part in sport's wider roles rather than just performing.

Mass participation and élite sport in Australia

Checkpoints

1 Active Australia is about promoting healthy lifestyles through participation in regular physical activity.

2 Australia has greater spaces for sport, a young population and a more favourable climate.

3 Geographical factors that may limit the scope of professional sport in Australia are the large distances between capital cities where most teams are based.

4 The AIS reflects the decentralising factors of the separate states in Australia in that each state has its own institute of sport offering support for élite athletes in that state.

Exam practice

In an attempt to establish Olympic success, after 1976 Australia set up a network of sports institutes, offering support and facilities for the top athletes. Élite athletes get sports-science support and state grants to allow full-time training. Medal winners are offered financial rewards. The sports search programme identifies potential talent, and widening participation means a larger pool of talent.

Revision checklist
The comparative study of global sporting systems

By the end of this chapter you should be able to:

1	Give an overview of sport in the USA.	Confident	Not confident **Revise** pages 108–109
2	Describe the historical development of sport and PE in the USA.	Confident	Not confident **Revise** pages 108–109
3	Explain how sport is administered in the USA.	Confident	Not confident **Revise** pages 110–111
4	Comment on the concept of mass participation in the USA.	Confident	Not confident **Revise** pages 112–113
5	Explain the structure of élite sport in the USA.	Confident	Not confident **Revise** pages 112–113
6	Give an overview of sport in Australia.	Confident	Not confident **Revise** pages 114–115
7	Describe the historical development of Australian sport and PE.	Confident	Not confident **Revise** pages 114–115
8	Describe the cultural background of Australian sport.	Confident	Not confident **Revise** pages 114–115
9	Explain how sport is administered in Australia.	Confident	Not confident **Revise** pages 116–117
10	Describe the structure and function of school and college sport in Australia.	Confident	Not confident **Revise** pages 116–117
11	Comment on the concept of mass participation in Australia.	Confident	Not confident **Revise** pages 118–119
12	Explain the structure of élite sport in Australia.	Confident	Not confident **Revise** pages 118–119

Resources

This section is intended to help you develop your study skills for examination success. You will benefit if you try to develop skills from the beginning of your course. Modern AS and A-level exams are not just tests of your recall of textbooks and your notes. Examiners who set and mark the papers are guided by assessment objectives that include skills as well as knowledge.

Exam board specifications

In order to organise your notes and revision you will need a copy of your exam board's syllabus specification. You can obtain a copy by writing to the board or by downloading the syllabus from the exam board's website.

AQA (Assessment and Qualifications Alliance)
Publications Department, Stag Hill House,
Guildford, Surrey GU2 5XJ
www.aqa.org.uk

EDEXCEL
190 High Holborn, London WC1V 7BH
www.edexcel.org.uk

OCR (Oxford, Cambridge and Royal Society of Arts)
1 Hills Road, Cambridge CB2 1GG
www.ocr.org.uk

WJEC (Welsh Joint Education Committee)
245 Western Avenue, Cardiff CF5 2YX
www.wjec.co.uk

The AS/A-level specifications

All A-level courses are in two parts, with a number of separate modules or units in each part. Students will start by studying the AS (Advanced Subsidiary). Those wishing to do so will go on to study the second part of the course, called A2. There is some element of choice as to which modules are studied but this may depend on the awarding body.

Advanced Subsidiary

The AS modules are compulsory and they cover the common core of the subject. AS is designed to provide appropriate assessment of the knowledge, understanding and skills expected of candidates who have completed the first half of a full A-level qualification. The level of demand of the AS exam is that expected of candidates halfway through a full A-level course of study, i.e. between GCSE and A level.

AS may be used in one of two ways:

→ As a final qualification, allowing you to broaden your studies and to defer a decision about specialism.
→ As the first half (50 per cent) of an A-level qualification, which must be completed before an A-level award can be made.

Thus, the AS specification establishes core principles on which an understanding of physical education and sport is based, and at the same time covers relevant topics in sufficient depth to form coherent modules for students who may not continue their study of physical education and sport to A level.

A level (AS + A2)

The A-level exam course is in two parts:

→ The AS is the first half of the course and constitutes 50 per cent of the total award. It will normally comprise three teaching and learning modules or units.
→ The A2 is the second half of the course, the remaining 50 per cent of the total award. It also normally comprises a further three teaching and learning modules or units which, in addition to introducing new knowledge, extend the core principles.

Each teaching and learning module will normally be assessed through an associated assessment unit.

The jargon

Every A-level specification includes *synoptic assessment* at the end of the A2 course. Synoptic questions draw on the ideas and concepts of earlier units and thus link topics. Synoptic assessment is dealt with in more detail on pages 126 to 127.

Assessment units

AS and A2 physical education and sport each comprise four assessment units or modules. In both AS and A2 one of the units is assessed by written examination taken at two specific times of the year, January and June. The second component in each case involves a method of practical assessment. Awarding Bodies use a combination of centre-assessed coursework and moderated practical sports assessment.

What are the main differences between AS and A2?

→ AS and A2 courses are designed so that the level of difficulty steadily increases, with the A2 containing the more demanding concepts.
→ In A2 there is much greater emphasis on the skills of application and analysis than in AS.
→ A2 includes synoptic assessment.

Modules and their shelf life

Any module can be retaken to improve your grade. You may resit any unit once during the time when the results are held in the Awarding Body's unit bank. When you decide to cash in for an AS/A-level award the Awarding Body will use the best result from each unit you have attempted. Any AS result can be converted into a full A-level award by taking the A2 exam at any time while the specification remains valid.

Assessment objectives

For AS and A level the scheme of assessment will test your ability in the following areas:

→ knowledge and understanding
→ application of knowledge and understanding, analysis, synthesis and evaluation
→ experiment and investigation
→ quality of written communication.

At A2 there is an additional category: synthesis of knowledge, understanding and skills. This is the synoptic element, where knowledge and skills from different modules are linked together and assessed.

Action point

Not all AS and A2 units are assessed in the January series of exams. Check with your teacher how and when you will be assessed.

Action point

Check with your teacher how your practical sports skills will be asessed.

Grade booster

The examination specification (formerly called the syllabus) is an extremely useful document. It clearly states the requirements for each topic you study. You should obtain your own copy, from your teacher, the internet, or by application to the relevant examination board (known as the Awarding Body). If you are not sure which Awarding Body to contact, your teacher will be able to help you.

Links

While the content of each of the modules at AS is self-contained, during the study of each module, opportunities should be taken to enable you to integrate different aspects of the subject. The link feature helps you to achieve this by highlighting connections between different chapters in the revision guide. The specification is designed to allow for the progression from AS to A level, both in terms of the difficulty of the topics and in the skill and understanding that are required.

Synoptic assessment

One of the aims of A2 assessment is to enable candidates to show knowledge and understanding of facts, principles and concepts from different areas of physical education and to make connections between them. You must understand what is meant by 'synoptic assessment' if you are to be fully prepared for your A2 examinations.

Synoptic assessment

This involves the drawing together of knowledge, understanding and skills learnt in the different units of the AS/A2 physical education course.

→ It may require you to apply knowledge of a number of areas of the course to a particular situation or context.
→ It may require you to use knowledge and understanding of principles and contexts in planning experimental work and in the analysis and evaluation of data.
→ It will take place at the end of your course.

Why do A2 exams contain a synoptic element?

Modular exams were introduced for a variety of reasons, one of which was to allow students to study a 'theme' in a manageable block of information.

However, in a modular course there is a tendency for candidates to gain success in a unit then forget the concepts they have learnt as soon as the exam has been taken.

Synoptic questions require you to transfer concepts from one unit to another and make connections.

Having an overview of the subject is thought to be a better preparation for higher education and employment.

Being able to link information gives you a greater understanding and is more satisfying and fulfilling, allowing you to contribute more effectively in problem-solving situations.

How can I gain synoptic skills?

Physical education is inherently cyclical and therefore synoptic in the world of sport coaches, managers and teachers who are constantly looking at many different ways of improving performance. You will have naturally applied many of these ideas and skills learnt during AS physical education and even your GCSE course! So, in studying A2 physical education you will have been using synoptic skills without realising it.

How can I prepare for synoptic questions?

→ From your specification, check out which module will contain synoptic questions.

→ Revise the basics of earlier modules and, as you do so, list topics that link with those you have recently studied at A2.

→ Carry out regular revision throughout the course.

→ Make use of past question papers, particularly specimen questions provided by your Awarding Body.

→ As you can expect to encounter new contexts which draw together different ideas, read generally around the subject and 'check the net'.

How are synoptic questions marked?

Examiners use the following criteria when they asses your synoptic answers:

→ **Practical links and examples** – try to back up each point you make with a specific sports example, the more detail the better.

→ **Theoretical links** – make references to named theories and research you have covered in all the modules you have studied.

→ **Analysis** – show that you understand the topic area by debating and challenging the issue in the question.

→ **Opinion and judgement** – don't be afraid to give your own feeling on the subject, and to relate an answer to your own experience in sport.

→ **Use of technical language** – try to incorporate as many technical terms as you can so long as they apply to the topic area. Don't forget to include a definition or explanation of the terms you use.

> **Action point**
>
> As you review your notes, make your own synoptic links.

> **Action point**
>
> Try to pick out the main synoptic topics for your specification. Produce and use a set of revision cards that answer the following points:
> → How does this issue/topic link to the other topics I have studied?
> → Can I link any theories, perspectives or research to this topic?
> → Can I identify a debate about this issue/topic?
> → Can I refer to specific examples or case studies linked to this issue/topic?

Study skills

This spread gives advice on taking notes during your studies and revision techniques to help you prepare for your exams.

Note taking

Note taking involves condensing speech or writing into an abbreviated form, which nevertheless contains the same essential information as the original. This skill is particularly important in the study of physical education and sport where there is a wide range of topics and subjects. The process of note taking requires you to concentrate on the essential information and in itself is an aid to learning. The second function of note taking is to provide you with an aid to future study and revision. It is much easier to refer back to and revise from notes that you have made yourself.

If you are a student attending classes you will probably make most of your notes during lessons and lectures, with your teacher being the main source of information. There are two pitfalls you must try to avoid: do not try to take down every word the teacher says, and when making notes from written sources do not copy out whole passages. The purpose of note taking is to produce a more manageable summary of the most important information.

The following are some points of general advice:

→ Use a looseleaf file so that you can add to or re-arrange your notes.
→ Space your notes out on the page so that you can add further information later.
→ Pick out key words or headings by underlining or using a highlighter pen.
→ Always write down book and page references in case you need to check back at a later date. Coursework assessment usually includes marks for including a reference section.
→ Don't forget to include quotes and the names of theories you come across.
→ Consider diagrams and flow charts as an alternative way of presenting information.

Reading

A-level success depends partly upon the ability to acquire and retain a wide range of knowledge. This is most effectively achieved by reading around the subject; class notes and a textbook alone are inadequate. Try to use more than one textbook as authors vary in their treatment of topics. There are also a number of excellent television programmes and video presentations on many of the topics covered in physical education and sport and these can also be useful sources of additional information.

Active revision

Start revising in good time; it will allow you to practise and develop the necessary skills to use in the exam. If you are studying other subjects, devise a plan where you use set times to study each subject.

Try to identify what you need to revise in terms of skills as well as topics. Completing a series of practice questions, such as those included in this guide, can be a good starting point in identifying any areas that you need to work on. Plan your revision on a week-by-week basis.

Review your plan regularly and adapt it as necessary. Some topics and activities will take more or less time than you anticipated. Build in opportunities for relaxation and fun in your schedule; breaks for fresh air and exercise will help your concentration.

Revision strategies

Use tables – these can help you organise information so that it can be used in different ways.

Discuss issues in your class

→ Have question-and-answer sessions with fellow students.
→ Ask a family member to test you on the key words for each unit.
→ Make audio tapes of key points and theories which you can play back when you are sitting on the bus or on your way to class – there is always time for revision!

Use examination questions

After you have revised a topic area it is vital that you are able to apply your knowledge and understanding in a critical way to an examination question. Whole questions may appear daunting at first. Try answering the shorter sub-questions or writing plans for the essay and synoptic questions.

Examiner's secrets

Tackle an unfamiliar question by applying your knowledge of relevant theories.

The benefits of using real questions

→ You become familiar with the style and language used in questions.
→ There will be popular questions which examine similar areas, even if the precise wording changes.
→ They provide a check on your understanding as well as your recall of knowledge.
→ They may reveal gaps in your knowledge and weaknesses in one or more topic areas; use this feedback to review your revision plan.
→ You can practise doing difficult questions.

Action point

Check out your examination board's website. Most include specimen exam papers and mark schemes which you can download.

Exam papers

At both AS and A level there is a considerable emphasis on understanding, interpreting and applying knowledge. In addition to the factual content, you will need to appreciate the underlying principles and apply these to sporting situations. This, and the information below, will better prepare you for the types of questions you will encounter on exam papers. It will also enable you to understand the principles involved.

Exam questions

Each module or unit will contain a number of structured questions, while some may also require you to answer a longer question or essay – this is often true of the A2 papers. There may be a choice of questions, but no more than one or two per module. Examiners spend a considerable amount of time preparing, revising and refining exam questions. The contents of each paper are agreed upon by a committeee after each question has undergone a thorough and rigorous analysis to minimise the chance of misinterpretation by the student.

During revision, when confronted with a mass of information, it is tempting to try to work out which topics are 'going to come up' and not revise certain topics. This is not a good idea with modular exams as the questions are designed to cover every topic outlined on the specification. You should be asking yourself what you should do with the knowledge that you have.

Structured questions

These are the most common types of questions used in AS and A-level physical education and sport exams. They usually require you to write at least a number of short sentences, although they can also include the opportunity for extended writing.

Remember that the mark allocation given to each question is a good guide in terms of how much the examiners are expecting you to write. Some exam boards combine the question and answer paper, and the space available for the answer to a question is another good indicator of how much writing you need to include in your answers.

Structured questions are often presented in several parts based around a common topic area. You may well experience an increase in the degree of difficulty as you work through the questions. The first part may be simple recall, perhaps defining a term. The most difficult part is often at the end and may ask you to give an opinion or analysis about an issue in physical education and sport. Very often, in physical education and sports questions, marks will be awarded for referring to practical sports examples. Many questions will actually state this, but it is good practice to back up any factual points you make with a practical sports example.

Action point

Do rough calculations of how much time to spend on questions for the papers you are sitting. Use these time allocations when practising answers and develop a confident view of how much you can write in that time.

Examiner's secrets

Examiners do not set out to trick you. Very often candidates may panic or not read the question sufficiently carefully, and so trick themselves.

Watch out!

Papers have inbuilt time for you to read the question carefully. This enables you to decide on which topic the question is focussing and highlight key words.

Watch out!

Where you have choice, always read through the whole of the question before deciding if that is the one for you.

Essay and higher-mark questions

All too often, students rush into essay and higher-mark questions, writing everything they know about the topic identified in the question. You need to take time with this type of question, first reading the question through several times to ensure you understand fully what it is that you are required to do. When you start such a question, plan or sketch out your answer. This will not only help you organise your answer logically but will also give you a checklist to which you can refer while writing out your final answer. In this way, you will be less likely to repeat yourself, wander off the subject or miss out important sections.

Very often, essay and higher-mark questions in physical education and sport will require debate or discussion of an issue. The trick here is to look to develop two sides of an argument. Sometimes, the argument required will be clearly evident in the question set; at other times, you may have the choice and need to develop your own debate.

A basic plan that could be used to answer an essay or higher-mark question could include the following:

→ **Intro** – set out how you are going to answer the question that the examiners have set.
→ **Key terminolgy** – introduce any key terms or theories you think relate to the question.
→ **Overview** – outline a basic background to the topic area. In a socio-cultural question this could include an historical overview of the issue. In a scientific question this may include an overview of the relevant theories and research.
→ **Case study/applied example** – can you relate the question to a specific practical sports example or specific case study or investigation you have covered?
→ **Answer to specific points** – does the question ask you to discuss and explain any areas in particular?
→ **Conclusion** – sum up the main points you have made in your answer. Can you finish with a personal opinion or view?

Grade booster

Where appropriate, use well-labelled diagrams. Even in essay-style questions this is an excellent way of communicating key points.

Exam papers (continued)

Key words in examinations

Exam questions use various words that key you in to how to approach them. A list of the words frequently used in exam questions, together with their approximate meanings, is given below.

Brief: A short statement of only the main points.

Calculate: Work out, showing all the stages in the derivation of the answer (your workings).

Compare: Write about the similarities and differences between two different topics or systems, e.g. school sport in one country compared to another named culture.

Define: State the meaning of, for example, a term without actually using the term itself.

Describe: A request for factual detail about a structure or process expressed logically and concisely.

Discuss: A critical account of various viewpoints and arguments in the topic set, drawing attention to their relative importance and significance. For example: discuss the advantages and disadvantages of a dedicated sports school system.

Evaluate: A judgement of evidence and/or arguments is required.

Explain: Describe and give reasons for.

Graphs: When a graph is being interpreted it is essential to relate any changes or trends. To plot a graph would require graph paper and some degree of accuracy. To sketch a graph requires only a rough outline.

Identify: Requires a word, phrase or brief statement. Show you recognise a concept or a theory in an item.

Illustrate: Include diagrams or drawings as much as possible *or* link to a specific practical example.

List: A sequence of numbered points one below the other with no further explanation.

Outline: Give only the main points. This means 'don't go into detail'. If you have learnt the topic thoroughly you may be tempted to waste time by writing too much!

State: A brief concise answer giving no reasons.

Suggest: There may be more than one explanation but as long as yours is reasonable it will gain some marks. This means that the question has no fixed answer and a wide range of reasonable responses is acceptable.

What is meant by: A definition is usually required. The amount of information to be included is dictated by the mark value.

Using past questions

You should make use of past papers, set by the Awarding Body whose exams you are taking, as preparation for your exams. Your school or college may provide you with past papers or you can write to the relevant Awarding Body or check out their website. Awarding Bodies also publish the mark schemes used by the examiners. These serve as an excellent guide to what is required on any particular topic.

At the end of each spread in this study guide there are exam questions, and the model answer to each question is given at the end of each section. You should attempt each question without reference to your notes, taking notice of the time allocation. After completing the question, mark it yourself. Your wording may not be quite the same but should contain the key words identified in the answer scheme. If you have not achieved a satisfactory answer, don't be too despondent. Check your notes and rewrite your answer. In this way, you will improve your understanding and learn from your mistakes. You will probably remember the right answer much better for having gone over it again.

Know the bodies and agencies that influence

It is useful to be able to include in your exam answers examples and facts about the various bodies that influence sport in the UK. Many of the questions in the socio-cultural units may ask direct questions about these bodies.

British Association of Sport and Exercise Sciences – aims to promote scientific study of sport and exercise in the UK.
More info: www.bases.org.uk

British Olympic Association – the national Olympic committee for Great Britain and Northern Ireland. They select and manage the Olympic teams as well as encourage participation at all levels and further the Olympic ideals within the country.
More info: www.boa.org.uk

British Paralympic Association – selects, funds and manages Great Britain's Paralympic team for the Paralympic Games. It is a registered charity whose core purpose is to create the best possible environment in which Britain's competitors can produce their lifetime's best performances.
More info: www.paralympics.org.uk

British Sports Trust – uses sport to develop skills for life through its Sports Leaders Awards. There are three awards specifically in sport and a fourth in basic expedition leadership.
More info: www.bst.org.uk

Central Council of Physical Recreation – acts as the voice of the national governing and representing bodies of sport and recreation in the UK. Speaks and acts to promote, protect and develop the interests of sport and physical recreation at all levels.
More info: www.ccpr.org.uk

Department for Education and Skills – the UK government department with responsibility for education including PE and sport in schools.
More info: www.dfes.gov.uk

Department of Culture, Media and Sport – the UK government department whose responsibility includes promoting and supporting all levels of sport and recreation.
More info: www.culture.gov.uk

English Federation of Disability Sport – the voice of disability sport in England. Launched in October 1999, it is the umbrella organisation for disabled sportsmen and women in the country. The EFDS seeks to represent all disabled people and works closely with the seven National Disability Sports Organisations (NDSOs).
More info: www.efds.co.uk

sport and recreation in the United Kingdom

Institute of Leisure and Amenity Management (ILAM) – the professional body for the leisure industry. Represents the interests of leisure managers across all sectors and specialisms of leisure.
More info: www.ilam.co.uk

National Coaching Foundation – the old name for SportCoach UK.

National Council for School Sport (NCSS) – the voice of school sport. The NCSS is a national forum body for school sport associations and others with an interest in school sport. Its main aim is to promote school sport opportunities for young people.
More info: www.ncss.org.uk

National Playing Fields Association (NPFA) – campaigns for and promotes the protection of playing fields across the UK. Now renamed Fields in Trust (FIT).
More info: www.npfa.co.uk

SportsAid (formerly known as the Sports Aid Foundation) – set up in 1998 and funded by the Foundation for Sport and the Arts, much of their funds come from the football pools. The organisation gives grants to developing athletes who are outside the World Class Programme.
More info: www.sportsaid.org.uk

Sport England – the lead sports development agency for England and the major distributor of the National Lottery sports fund. Its aim is to foster a healthier and more successful nation through increased investment in sport and active recreation. Other agencies in the UK are: Sports Scotland, Sport Cymru and the Northern Ireland Sports Council.
More info: www.sportengland.org.uk

Women's Sport Foundation (WSF) – funded through the sports councils, its aim is to promote female involvement in sport at all levels. It runs schemes to encourage female participants as well as raising the profile of élite female performers.
More info: www.wsf.org.uk

Youth Sports Trust – a registered charity established in 1994 with the aim of building a brighter future for young people in sport. Its main influence has been through the management of TOPs and Millennium Volunteer Programmes. It also supports schools that have specialist sports college status and those involved in the School Sport Coordinators programme.
More info: www.youthsporttrust.org

Know the strategies, schemes and sports bodies

It is useful to be able to include in your exam answers examples and facts about the various bodies that influence sport globally. Many of the questions in the socio-cultural units may ask direct questions about these bodies.

Able Aussie – target group programme coordinated by the ASC to raise the profile of disabled sport in Australia.

Active Australia – a national framework of mass participation, set up in 1916 and coordinated by the ASC.

Australian Council for Heath, Physical Education and Recreation – a national professional association representing people who work in the areas of health education, physical education, recreation, sport, dance, community fitness and movement sciences. The mission of the council is to promote healthy lifestyles for all Australians and particularly to study and promote its areas of focus.
More info: www.achper.org.au

Australian Football League (AFL) – governing body of Australian Rules Football, Americanised in recent years through a franchise programme and annual draft.

Australian Institute of Sport – based in Canberra, the federal capital, and set up in 1981, creates a central training base for Australia's top athletes.

Australian Sports Commission (ASC) – the body that coordinates sport across Australia, and is enriching the lives of all Australians through sport. It is responsible for both increasing participation and developing sports excellence in Australia.

Aussie Sport – a programme of sports with modified rules to encourage young people to participate in sporting activity.

that influence and affect sport in the cultures you have studied

Fundamental Motor Skills – a programme launched in the state of Victoria, Australia. It gave all primary school teachers access to a resource pack that taught young children ten basic motor skills required for sport.

Indigenous Sports programme – developed by the ASC in Australia to encourage more of the indigenous people to participate in active recreation. Major initiatives include the desert sport carnivals and the Arrafura Games.

Le Plein Air – a popular philosophy in France and one that permeates much of the sport for all and educational programmes.

National Collegiate Athletic Association (NCAA) – the body responsible for inter-college sport in the USA, also coordinates the athletic scholarship programme.

Sport Education in Physical Education Program (SEPEP) – a curriculum model for use in school physical education programmes in Australia. SEPEP relies on teachers and students to create a particular form of social system within physical education lessons known as student-centred learning.

Sport Pour Tous – French sports system with a similar concept to Sport for All, aimed at improving the health of the nation.

Title IX – federal legislation in the USA that promotes equal opportunity in terms of gender in school and college sport.

United States Olympic Committee (USOC) – the national Olympic committee for the USA. It selects and manages the Olympic teams as well as encouraging participation at all levels and furthering the Olympic ideals within the country. It is unique in that it does receive federal funding.

Glossary

Access

being able to take part in sport.

Adenosine triphosphate (ATP)

the basic unit of energy within the body. It is the end product of each of the three main energy systems.

Aerobic

requiring oxygen.

Agility

a fitness component that combines speed and flexibility.

All-or-none law

a neurone or muscle fibre either responds completely or not at all to a stimulus.

Americanisation

where American trends and attitudes invade traditional culture.

American Dream

the idea that in the USA anyone can rise from rags to riches.

Arousal

degree of mental readiness before a performance.

Autonomous phase

the final stage of skill development where all performance skills are mastered and other performance factors can be practised.

Axon

nerve fibre carrying messages away from the nerve cell body.

Blood doping

an illegal ergogenic aid where athletes withdraw a quantity of blood some weeks before a competition and then re-inject this blood just before competition.

Booster clubs

community clubs made up of old boys and local businessmen that provide financial support to school and college teams.

Boycott

the refusal of a country to compete in an event, usually for political reasons.

Broken-time payments

clubs paid working-class players the wages they could not earn while playing.

Capillaries

microscopic blood vessels that deliver oxygenated blood to the tissues via diffusion.

Capillarisation

the development of the capillary network in a part of the body. Includes increasing the absolute number of capillaries and the capillary density.

Carbohydrate loading

diet manipulation aimed at increasing the muscles' glycogen stores before a sports event.

Cardiac output

the amount of blood pumped by the heart per minute.

Centre of gravity

the point around which the various body parts can be said to be in balance.

Coactors

individuals performing the same task, but independently.

Cognitive phase

the first stage of skill development which covers task familiarisation and some basic practice.

Concentric

muscle contraction where the muscle creates force while shortening in length.

Cool-down

last stage of training and/or competition where the body should gradually reduce physical activity to resting levels.

Cue

a signal for some particular action – may be verbal, visual or kinaesthetic.

Displacement

the distance an object has moved in a given direction.

DOMS

(delayed onset of muscle soreness) condition affecting the muscle that results in localised pain following strenuous exercise.

Draft system

the system where professional teams select the best college players once a year.

Eccentric

a muscle creating force while the fibres are lengthening.

EPOC

(excess post-exercise oxygen consumption) the extra oxygen needed to restore the body to its pre-exercise state.

Ergogenic aid

any method employed by an athlete to improve performance.

Fatigue

depletion of the body's energy stores.

Franchise

a business agreement set up to maximise profit.

Glucose

the simplest form of carbohydrate and the basic ingredient for anaerobic and aerobic glycolysis.

Glycogen

the stored form of glucose, found in the muscles and liver.

Glycolysis

the breakdown of glucose.

Hypertrophy

increase in muscle bulk due to an increase in the cross-sectional area of the muscle fibres.

Interval

a period of work in a training session.

Intrinsic

description of motives that lie within an individual's control.

Lactate

toxic by-product of anaerobic glycolysis.

Lombardian ethic

named after the famous Green Bay Packers' most successful coach Vince Lombardi, who developed the idea that winning is the most important thing.

Maximum oxygen uptake

the measure of the maximum amount of oxygen that the body can use for each kilogram of body weight in one minute, also referred to as VO_2 max.

Mitochondria

the powerhouse of the cell where the Krebs cycle and electron transport system generates ATP.

Momentum

the product of mass and velocity ($M = mv$). It is a vector quantity and can be considered as a measure of the quantity of motion possessed by a body.

Motor unit

a nerve and its connecting muscle fibres.

Myoglobin

the oxygen-carrying agent within the muscle cell.

Onset of blood lactate accumulation (OBLA)

the point at which blood lactate levels suddenly increase, also referred to as lactate threshold.

PARQ

Physical Activity Readiness Questionnaire completed before training or testing to ensure that athletes are physiologically and psychologically prepared.

Peers

people who mix in the same environment, often of the same age.

Phosphocreatine

an energy-rich compound that is used by the body to create explosive energy.

Plyometrics

a method of fitness training that employs skipping and bounding actions to maximise power gains through isotonic eccentric muscle contractions.

Point of insertion

usually moves during muscle action.

Point of origin

remains relatively fixed during muscle action.

Proprioceptive neuromuscular facilitation (PNF)

usually performed with a partner and involves a pattern of alternating contraction and relaxation of the muscles being stretched.

Reaction time

the time taken to begin movement in response to a stimulus.

Recovery

the period following physical activity in which the body's systems repair damaged tissue and replenish energy stores.

Scalar quantity

physical quantity that is described completely in terms of its magnitude.

Schema

a mental framework or outline developed through past experience.

Self-efficacy

where an individual believes they have the ability to perform at a specified level in a certain task.

Significant other

a person who a performer relates to and holds in high esteem.

Social loafing

where an individual loses motivation within a group, linked to a loss of identity.

Target zone

a specific level of intensity that an athlete needs to work at to obtain a specific physiological adaptation.

Tidal volume

the amount of air moved each time we breathe, usually about 500ml.

Training zone

the zone within which it is necessary to have the heart rate to achieve a desired training effect.

Velocity

the rate at which a body moves. It is a vector quantity in that it possesses both magnitude and direction.

Vicarious experience

experiences gained by watching other people perform.

Vital capacity

the total amount of air that can be expired from the lungs after a maximum inhalation.

Further reading

General textbooks

Carnell, D., Ireland, J., et al. (2002) *Advanced PE for OCR AS* Heinemann

Honeybourne, J. (2003) *Btec National Sport* Nelson Thornes

Honeybourne, J., M. Hill and H. Moors (2004) *Advanced PE and Sport* 3rd Edn Nelson Thornes

Reference books

Adair, D. (1997) *Sport in Australian History*, Oxford University Press

Bailey, S. and W. Vamplew (1999) *100 Years of Physical Education 1899–1999* PEA

Clegg, C. (1995) *Exercise Physiology and Functional Anatomy* Feltham Press

Cox, R., G. Jarvie and W. Vamplew (2000) *Encyclopedia of British Sport* ABC-Clio

Danials, S. and A. Tedder (2000) *A Proper Spectacle – Women Olympians 1900–1936* ZeNaNa Press

Gill, D.L. (1986) *Psychological Dynamics of Sport* Human Kinetics

Gutmann, A. (1994) *The Olympics – A History of the Modern Games*, University of Illinois Press

Kent, M. (1998) *Oxford Dictionary of Sports Science and Medicine* 2nd Edn Oxford University Press

Money, T. (1987) *Manly and Muscular Diversions* The Bath Press

Schmidt, R.A. (1991) *Motor Learning and Performance* Human Kinetics

Seeley, R.R., Stephens, T.D. and P. Tate (1995) *Essentials of Anatomy and Physiology* Mosby

Sharp, R. (1992) *Acquiring Skill in Sport* Sports Dynamics

Wilmore, J.H. and D.L. Costhill (1999) *Physiology of Sport and Exercise* 2nd Edn Human Kinetics

Useful websites

www.ausport.gov.au

www.pe4u.co.uk

www.teachpe.com

www.physicaleducation.co.uk

www.uksport.gov.uk

www.youthsporttrust.org

This is not a prescriptive list and any further reading should be carried out after consultation with your teacher.

Index